Latin America's New Knowledge Economy:

Higher Education, Government,
and International Collaboration

Latin America's New Knowledge Economy:

Higher Education, Government, and International Collaboration

EDITED BY JORGE BALÁN

Seventh in a Series of Global Education Research Reports

New York

IIE publications can be purchased at: www.iiebooks.org

The Institute of International Education
809 United Nations Plaza, New York, New York 10017

Library of Congress Cataloging-in-Publication Data

Latin America's new knowledge economy : higher education, government, and international
collaboration / edited by Jorge Balán.
     pages cm
  ISBN 978-0-87206-358-7 (alk. paper)
  1. Education, Higher--Latin America. 2. Education and state--Latin America. 3. Education
and globalization--Latin America. 4. International cooperation. I. Balán, Jorge, 1940-
  LA543.L36 2013
  378.8--dc23
                              2012047301

The views expressed in these chapters are solely those of the authors.
They do not necessarily represent the official positions of the
Institute of International Education or the AIFS Foundation.

Series editors:
Daniel Obst, Deputy Vice President for International Partnerships, IIE
Sharon Witherell, Director of Public Affairs, IIE

Managing Editor: Daniel Obst, Luke Epplin
Consultant Editor: Shepherd Laughlin
Copy Editor: Teresa Barensfeld

Cover and text design: Pat Scully Design. Cover photo: São Paulo, Brazil.

Table of Contents

Figures and Tables

Forewords

By Allan E. Goodman

On a recent visit to Latin America, it became increasingly clear to me that leaders and policymakers in both the public and private sector are committed to investing in higher education to develop their workforce and future leaders.

This is certainly the case in Brazil, where President Dilma Rousseff has created a multiyear scholarship program called Ciência sem Fronteiras (known in English as the Brazil Scientific Mobility Program) to send 75,000 fully funded Brazilian students abroad for training in the science, technology, engineering, and math (STEM) fields, with an additional 26,000 scholarships expected to be funded by the private sector. These new scholarships—which *The Economist* has called "Brazil's boldest attempt to move up an economic gear"—are specifically targeted to produce a workforce that is trained in STEM fields and has the language and cultural skills needed to succeed in the workplace.

At a time when Brazil's economy is expanding rapidly, and Brazil and the United States are forging unprecedented ties in trade, energy, and scientific development, business leaders have joined in this effort, in the belief that these two countries should seek much stronger cooperation in higher education. Companies like Boeing, Cargill, and GE have been eager to contribute scholarships and offer internships to connect with these students and the colleges and universities that host them. We are also beginning to see increased interest in investing in education and training in Chile, Argentina, Mexico, and other countries as well, among leaders who seek to build the knowledge economy in their countries and to increase cooperation between Latin America and the United States.

As outlined in a chapter by Deputy Assistant Secretary of State Meghann Curtis, the Obama administration has also made it a priority to expand academic exchanges between Latin America and the United States, and the U.S. Department of State is implementing a number of programs to help meet these goals.

IIE is planning an expanded series of university fairs in 2013 that will bring U.S. universities together with STEM students in Brazil, Mexico, and Chile. With STEM education so key to economic development and building human capacity in their home countries, it is increasingly important to help foster an interest in pursuing further education in STEM fields and connect students with the institutions that best suit their needs.

We hope these chapters will help educators and policymakers to gain a broader understanding of new developments in Latin American higher education so that they may productively engage in mutually beneficial educational relationships.

Allan E. Goodman

President & CEO, Institute of International Education

BY WILLIAM L. GERTZ

All signs point to a marked increase in student educational exchange opportunities between the United States and the countries of Latin America. This increase will be fueled by economic development and social change throughout Latin America, as well as rapid demographic change in the United States.

First and foremost is the improving economic situation. According to the International Monetary Fund, Latin America's economy will grow 3.7 percent in 2012 and 4.1 percent in 2013. A growing middle class means that more Latin American students have the resources to attend U.S. colleges and universities. According to *Open Doors*, Mexico, Brazil, Columbia, and Venezuela rank within the top 25 places of origin for international students attending U.S. universities, with a combined total of 35,498 in the 2011/12 academic year.

We also see this impact at the secondary level, where participation has increased and demand is unprecedented. The American Institute For Foreign Study (AIFS) and our Foundation have experienced significant increases among Latin American students for our J-1 visa programs. More than 1,000 students from Latin America participate in our Au Pair in America and Academic Year in America cultural exchange programs, with the highest representation being from Brazil, Columbia, and Mexico.

More Latin American students are also participating in AIFS summer opportunities at the primary and middle school levels, and we expect this growth to continue. Students from Mexico, Honduras, Argentina, Costa Rica, and Venezuela attend our Summer Institute for the Gifted academic camp programs.

Latin America's economic development has helped to stabilize the region politically and socially, which has helped to increase its popularity as a study abroad destination. Additionally, the rapid growth of the Hispanic population in the United States is contributing to greater study-abroad participation in Latin America. According to the U.S. Census Bureau, there are now more than 52 million Americans of Hispanic descent, and Spanish is now spoken by over 12 percent of the population. Spanish language proficiency is becoming a necessity in the United States, and cultural and language immersion are the most effective means to achieve this end.

AIFS has seen significant growth among U.S. students studying on our programs in Chile, Peru, Costa Rica, and Brazil. We are expanding our Latin American opportunities and have just inaugurated a program in Buenos Aires. As we expand our institutional relationships throughout Latin America, AIFS will continue to develop international educational programs focused on language, history, culture, business, and ecology.

We are pleased to once again partner with the Institute of International Education on our continuing Global Education Research Reports.

William L. Gertz

President and CEO, American Institute For Foreign Study (AIFS)
Trustee, AIFS Foundation

Latin American Higher Education Systems in a Historical and Comparative Perspective

Jorge Balán, Columbia University

Higher education has undergone impressive growth and change over the last few decades in Latin America. This book selectively reviews some dimensions of this transformation, discussing policies, institutions, and programs, as well as their outcomes in terms of access, workforce training, and research. Individual chapters, commissioned from specialists from Latin America and the United States, stand as original, independent contributions focusing on key issues in higher education: changes in institutional autonomy and system governance, the contributions of higher education to advanced workforce development, policy responses to the continuing challenges of access and equity, government-sponsored study-abroad scholarships programs in several countries, trends in academic mobility and its outcomes for brain drain and gain, the changing landscape of U.S. universities' and corporations' investment in the region, and recent development of U.S. government exchange programs with Latin America.

The chapters of this book consider the region as a whole or compare selected countries, with the important exception of chapters 8 and 9, devoted to explaining Brazilian success in building research universities and including an interview with

Brazil's Minister of Education about the large-scale science and engineering fellowship program launched in 2011 to promote stronger linkages with research universities in more advanced countries. Brazil, a country of continental proportions but a latecomer to higher education, is now responsible for producing well over one-half of all research and doctoral degrees in the region. The Appendix to the volume brings a summary view of IIE's work in Latin America.

This Introduction provides a brief historical and comparative context for the book through a discussion of the long-term process leading to the consolidation of mass institutional systems of higher education, considering intraregional variations, noticing differences with other regions of the world, and reflecting on the major dilemmas faced by public policy in higher education in the last decade.

The Emergence and Growth of National Educational Systems

There were about 25 universities in Spanish America early in the 19th century, when the new republics won their independence from the Spanish crown, but none had been built in Brazil under Portuguese rule. Although they could hardly be regarded as distinguished by European standards, colonial authorities, under the influence of the French Enlightenment during the second half of the 18th century, had counted on those universities, regulated by government, to serve public needs rather than to follow their own corporative interests or those of the Church (Ruegg, 2004). The new republics were to continue this tradition, although for several decades after independence university life was disrupted or entirely discontinued by wars, political upheaval, and severe fiscal constraints.

The first republican innovations in higher education were adopted in Chile and Uruguay in the 1840s, to be followed decades later by many other nations looking to renew university life when political conditions and an increase in public resources allowed them to focus on education. New universities were designed to coordinate public education systems along centralized Napoleonic lines. This ambitious goal was eventually to be delegated to ministries of education—the *Universidad de la Republica* in Uruguay remained responsible for secondary education until the 1920s—but national universities maintained through modern times a public mission closely linked to the state. Legal frameworks gave the public university a special status and protection to fulfill such mission-limiting interference from government, still responsible for its funding through the regular annual budget.

Export-led economic growth in the late 19th and early 20th centuries was conducive to the expansion in the number and size of national universities. Rapid urbanization, the emergence of the modern middle class, and the increase in state revenues originated in foreign trade fueled the ambitions of enlightened political elites that regarded universities as symbols of modernity. The Southern Cone countries—Argentina, Chile, Uruguay, and southern Brazil—and other nations such as Costa Rica and Cuba were among the main beneficiaries of the expansion in global trade and in transatlantic immigration, and they enjoyed an earlier start and faster growth of mass public education. Immigrants with higher levels of education than the population of the receiving countries fostered both the demand for education and the supply of teachers and university professionals.

In Spanish America central governments often took over provincial institutions or those run by religious orders to build or reconstruct new universities; whereas in Brazil the state of São Paulo competed with the federation to launch the first universities in the 1930s on the basis of preexisting professional schools. By the 1950s there were around 150 universities in the 20 Latin American republics, with a total of about half a million students. The large majority of these students attended public universities that made up the core of the still relatively small and poorly coordinated higher education systems. Argentina's eight national universities made up the largest system, accounting for almost one-third of the total, following the rapid expansion of student numbers with the first centralized experiment in open admissions and the opening of a technological university (Levy, 1986, p. 340).

National policies favored organizational homogeneity and curricular standardization. Universities were bureaucratically regulated by ministries of education with limited or no capacity to influence curricula, faculty appointments and promotion, student admission, and the selection of presidents and deans. However, breaks with university autonomy were not uncommon, as in Argentina between 1947 and 1955. Over time, universities became autonomously run state institutions with a delegated state monopoly to grant professional degrees.

Public universities are often described as confederations of *facultades*, each of them in charge of degree-granting programs giving direct access to the most prestigious, state-regulated, and licensed professions. Private universities, authorized early in Chile and Brazil, were delegated to have similar state functions but enjoyed greater freedom in administration, governance, and finance, while only occasionally receiving a direct public subsidy. Close links with the national and provincial political elites made universities a part of the political scene, as key agents in the political socialization and recruitment of the youth. Very often these highly politicized universities were important actors in opposition politics.

Professional schools, or *facultades*—in particular, law, medicine, and engineering, often predating the official founding of a university—were the key organizational units, enjoying much independence from the central university administration and responsible for teaching programs leading to professional degrees. New schools were created as new professions became regulated by the state (e.g., public accounting, dentistry, pharmacy, architecture, and psychology). Part-time instructors, usually practicing professionals, were in charge of teaching programs characterized by their rigid structure and long duration. Almost totally dependent on public subsidies, university funding was politically negotiated in detailed annual budgets approved by their countries' legislatures.

Basic sciences and the humanities were typically relegated to schools adopting similar curricular formats and aiming to achieve professional status through admission into new licensed professions (i.e., secondary school teaching). Attached to each school one would find hospitals and clinics, laboratories, services of all kinds, programs of popular education, and many other ancillary activities. However, professional education remained the key mission of the university beyond the often voiced ambition of being a center of intellectual debate, a locus for academic research and scholarship, and a forum for public debate on national issues. Applied research, technological innovation, and links with industrial and agricultural sectors were unusual, as they were perceived to be most properly the function of autonomous government institutes and laboratories outside of the university. Teacher training took place until the 1950 in special secondary schools and later on in postsecondary institutions outside, or at the margins, of the more prestigious universities.

Following the European tradition, university study was tuition-free or had low fees, and it was in many cases a part-time activity carried out under the supervision of part-time faculty. The residential campus in the Anglo-American tradition was more the exception than the rule, while it was not unusual for students to work and study at a slower pace than planned in the official programs. A few universities achieved regional and international recognition in some areas, indicated by the acceptance of their graduates in European and North American universities and by their ability to attract foreign scholars who played a key role in building a research tradition in newly founded universities such as La Plata in Argentina in the 1910s and São Paulo in Brazil in the 1930s. Segregated from the national educational systems—many running their own preparatory schools—universities were yet dependent upon the expansion of mass systems of public education that generated growing student demand.

Historians have recently documented how the region fitted within global trends in literacy and schooling since the 1870s, showing the early origins and persistent gap with the more advanced economies in the world. Studies have shown that the role of compulsory mass schooling was promoted by the nation-states in the 18th and 19th centuries, first by several German states, then by other European countries, a majority of states in the United States, and a number of Latin American countries, although free and compulsory education was often more a utopian project than a reflection of a reality in this region (Benavot, Resnik, & Corrales, 2000, p. 11). The Latin American projects still come up against fiscal constraints, poor transportation and communications, limited trade with isolated regions, a lack of national monetary integration, and the overall weakness of national institutions. The implementation of mandatory schooling laws has proven to be a difficult, long-term process, still incomplete today in many countries that have extended its scope to include some or all of secondary education but are unable to provide the conditions for a majority of young people to complete the mandatory cycle. Access to public schools, as well as their quality, was and still is very uneven, with striking differences between regions, rural and urban areas, and the rich and the poor. Arguably the greatest success over time has been in ironing out gender differences in access and graduation, with the exception of a few countries, while some of the consistent long-term failures were encountered by educational policies designed for the indigenous population.

Throughout Spanish America mass educational systems became centralized, as control over them was removed from the municipalities. Private schools did not receive public support, although they were often strictly regulated by the central authorities (Newland, 1994). Centralization was justified on the perceived need to build a unified nation out of a variety of regional autonomies, diverse ethnic and linguistic groups, and recent immigration that brought in different cultures and religions. Fiscal resources were also centralized, since financing of the public sector was largely based on taxes levied by the national government on foreign trade. National governments controlled the funds to build the school system, employ teachers and administrators, and manage the bureaucracy. Education became a key line within federal budgets and a major source of public employment in systems often ridden with clientelism and political patronage. In some countries, the provinces or states, often those with more resources, maintained their own systems with little coordination with the federal government. Centralized educational systems fostering homogeneity had a serious bias in favor of the more developed areas and the urban population. Brazil was a major exception since it had a decentralized educational system based upon its federal structure. The relative ability of states to raise funds through taxation of foreign trade, however, strongly reinforced regional disparities in education.

The increase of literacy rates among the adult population during the first half of the 20th century, a crude indicator of the impact of mass education, shows impressive growth for the whole region but also the persistent differences between early movers, who benefitted the most from the expansion of global trade before 1930, and the other nations. Argentina, Chile, and Uruguay stood well above the mean both in 1900 and 1950. A second group of smaller countries, Costa Rica, Cuba, and Panama, joined them by the latter date. Nearly half of the adult population of the two most populous countries, Mexico and Brazil, remained illiterate by 1950, while literacy was even more restricted in the poorer Central and South American countries (Benavot & Riddle, 1988; Newland, 1994). Regional inequalities within countries were also of great magnitude, with Brazil as a striking example. Although even poorer states showed an increase in elementary school attendance, by 1940 enrollment rates in the South were over 40 percent of the school age population, two or three times larger than in the Northeast (Martínez-Fritscher, Musacchio, & Viarengo, 2010).

The initial phase of economic globalization, from the 1870s to World War I, saw a strong push to increase mass schooling not only throughout the West and its offshoots, but also in Japan. Such a push, however, was more restricted and generally less successful in Latin America. There was considerable convergence in educational achievement in Europe. Somewhat less advanced countries, such as Australia, Ireland, and New Zealand, caught up with Western Europe at this time. However, Latin America did not reduce the gap despite the overall growth in mandatory schooling (Morrisson & Murtin, 2009, p. 32). Only the most educationally advanced countries, such as Argentina, Uruguay, and Chile, saw the gap reduced with Southern and Eastern Europe, the countries where a majority of their immigrants originated.

Australia and Argentina, both European offshoots, provide contrasting examples of the limitations of the Latin American centralized model. Australia, starting with very low levels of educational achievement up to the 1850s, caught up with the United States and Canada at the eve of the 20th century and continued along a similar line of educational expansion ever since. Argentina, with starting levels comparable to Australia, having enacted free and compulsory schooling laws in the 1870s, did not benefit as much educationally from the economic growth brought about by the expansion of world trade, consistently lagging behind Australia (and the United States) in average years of schooling until today. Decentralization and better public and private funding allowed a greater reach of mass schooling and less inequality in Australia than in Argentina, well before their growth patterns started to diverge in the second half of the 20th century (Morrisson & Murtin, 2009).

Ewout Frankema, in his recent study of the expansion of mass education in Latin America during the last century, argued that primary school enrollment rates and average number of years of schooling, both of which rose consistently throughout the period, are poor indicators of progress without considering also grade enrollment and school completion data (Frankema, 2009, p. 362). Even after achieving full primary school enrollment rates by the 1960s, it took several decades for Latin American countries to cope with grade repetition and precompletion dropout rates, strong indicators of low-quality standards in basic education. His analysis supports the widely held view about the backwardness and unequal distribution of basic education in Latin America compared to East Asian countries, factors that constrained economic growth in the former region. By 1960, only 7 percent of adults in Latin America completed secondary education, while in East Asia 11 percent did so. The gap had increased four decades later, when the corresponding figures were 18 percent and 44 percent (Vegas & Petrow, 2008).

The early development of mass educational systems in Latin America reflected inequalities in the distribution of wealth, income, and opportunities that became barriers to the universalization of mandatory schooling. The gap between regions and between rural and urban areas within each country, strongly associated with those between social classes and ethnic groups, was not reduced through centralized educational policies that typically resulted in greater subsidies to the more advantaged groups. Although the university sector proved to be a channel for social mobility, its role was seriously constrained by the selectivity operating in earlier educational cycles as well as by the location of universities in the richer cities and regions and the organization of undergraduate programs in long professional cycles. Probably unaware of their socioeconomic elitism—because loose admission systems and tuition-free studies made possible a minority representation of the children of the urban working and lower middle classes—the lack of institutional competition and limited professionalization of academic life made universities also unaware of their academic mediocrity.

Reforms, Upheaval, and the Consolidation of Mass Education Systems

By the mid-20th century, the Latin American university model had been well established.[1] In the following decades, the limitations of this model were becoming evident as these countries faced the challenges of industrialization, urbanization, expanded access to public education, and the growing and more diverse demands from students and the labor market. The joint challenges of the recurrent fiscal crises of the state— the inability to meet all the competing demands, including the public provision of free education at all levels, while being unable or unwilling to raise the level of taxation—and the political friction among governments, the university administrations, and the student movement, often resulted in university crises of major proportions.

The period between 1950 and 1975—the culmination of the import-substitution industrialization process initiated in the 1930s, with marked cycles and high inflation—saw many attempts to modernize and reform the national universities from within (Levy, 2005). Under the leadership of groups of faculty, students and administrators, the universities sought to achieve transformations that would make the institutions better suited to serve the new national development projects, often convinced of the role of scientific and technological research and of the new social sciences in industrialization and economic development. Organizational reforms were assumed to run parallel to a reorientation of research and teaching within the university. These reforms, often inspired by the Anglo-Saxon model that become highly visible after the war and was promoted by international aid agencies, included the professionalization and full-time involvement of a research-oriented faculty, curriculum changes in undergraduate programs to make them more flexible and student-driven, formalization of a graduate cycle of studies, and strengthening of discipline-based departments and the central administration (with the abolition of traditional academic chairs and erosion of the independence of professional schools within the university; Levy, 2005).

The widening political gap between the autonomous public universities and democratically elected governments was made more critical by a radicalized student activism in the Cold War climate of the latter half of the 20th century. The most visible confrontations took place in the late 1960s, a time of student mobilization worldwide. These protests were very frequent throughout the period in most countries in Latin America, reinforcing the image of a politically involved student movement, even if it was often fostered by the mobilization of a minority of student activists with representation in university governance and closely linked to national political movements and parties. In many cases, student confrontations with the authorities mixed radical demands for revolutionary change with more limited demands for organizational transformation and more generous funding.

Reform and expansion, always difficult to achieve, required considerably more resources than what governments were ready to bring to the table. Universities tended to be permanently and seriously underfunded, yet their administrations were reluctant to make difficult choices between the pressure to open student admissions and that for organizational reforms. Governments, with extremely limited capacity to intervene in university life and unable or unwilling to commit further public resources to traditional universities unresponsive to their views, sought different paths to foster national capacities in science and technology. Within the university sector, their option was to build new institutions rather than to support the reforms of those over which they had no control. Furthermore, central governments strengthened new agencies to fund and coordinate scientific and technological research and to support development projects, laboratories, and applied research institutes outside of the university sector, with only limited commitment to the universities and thus reduced impact upon their reform.

The suspension of university autonomy by authoritarian governments became widespread throughout the region during the Cold War period. Policies of these regimes varied from country to country, and often evolved over time within the same nation. Thus, in Argentina, the 1966 military intervention resulted in a massive brain drain from the public university, only to be followed a few years later by a government plan to strengthen the diversification of the higher education sector through a system of new public universities outside the main cities and a short-lived reform of their academic organization. Another military coup in Argentina in 1976, on the contrary, radically reduced funding to the public universities, limited student admission, persecuted politically adverse students and faculty, and eliminated academic freedom over a period of several years without launching any new initiative for the public sector. The Pinochet regime in Chile (1973–1990) after several years of highly repressive measures launched in the early 1980s ambitious, market-friendly reforms, leading to a diversified, yet academically controlled, higher education system in consonance with the decentralization and privatization of primary and secondary education. Another striking example was the military regime in Brazil (1964–1985), which also went through different phases to introduce some long-term reforms in graduate education and in research funding (see chapter 8 by Balbachevsky in this volume).

An approach to cope with demands for greater access without committing further public funds throughout the region was the change in policy toward the sector of private universities initiated in the 1950s (Levy, 1986). Although policies differed greatly from country to country (with the private sector making early inroads in Chile, Brazil, and Colombia), the overall process of growth in the private sector is perhaps the most outstanding feature of higher education transformation in the region, greatly accelerated in the last few decades.

Privatization encompasses many dimensions. Student enrollment and the number of institutions in the private sector are the most visible ones, although the proportion of funding that originated in private spending is perhaps the most important figure from a public policy perspective. Organisation for Economic Co-operation and Development (OECD) data indicate that in 2009 household expenditures accounted for 68.1 percent of total spending in tertiary education in Chile, the highest rate in the world, while in neighboring Argentina they accounted for only 12.9 percent, toward the low end of the distribution (OECD, 2012, table B3.2b). These numbers indicate the wide range exhibited within Latin America, yet they correspond to countries with relatively similar levels in GDP per capita and in average educational attainment.

Nancy Birdsall and her colleagues at the Inter-American Development Bank (Birdsall, 1996; Birdsall, Ross, & Sabot, 1997) have looked at the relative weight of public spending in higher education compared to basic education as an element in the unequal distribution of public subsidies and a key dimension responsible for the differences in average educational achievement in the region when compared to East Asia. Along similar lines, Frankema has shown that the ratio of public expenditure per student enrolled in tertiary to primary education in Latin America or sub-Saharan Africa was, in the 1950s and 1960s, much higher than in Western Europe or in Asia (Frankema, 2009, table 4). The ratio declined on the average for Latin America, from 15:1 in the 1960s to 5.6:1 in the 1990s, but it still was relatively high in international comparisons.

Rapidly increased enrollments in higher education with slower growth in public and private resources—as was the case with primary and secondary education earlier—may be held responsible for a decline in quality, including lower graduation rates and longer term-to-degree periods among those who do graduate. Quantitative expansion with a loss in quality is perhaps the most widespread burning issue of education at all levels in Latin America, but it has been better documented in primary and secondary than in higher education. Underfunding of education, however, is not the only culprit for poor quality. A recent report card for education in the region, entitled

Quantity Without Quality, praises Latin American governments for the fiscal effort of the last two decades, yet indicates that the quality problem has persisted due to a lack of focus on learning outcomes and accountability:

> Latin America has significantly increased public spending on education and has managed to get many more children into school. Over the past decade, the percentage of children entering and completing primary and secondary education has risen faster in Latin America than in any other part of the developing world. This is no small achievement and reflects the commitment of successive governments to extend basic education to as many children as possible. But the region has made almost no progress in improving learning and in reducing inequality in its schools. Latin America scores at the bottom on every global test of student achievement. Children from poor families routinely score much lower than children from middle and upper class families. Despite sincere and impressive efforts to reform, most schools still fail to provide children with the skills and competencies they need for economic and personal success and active citizenship. (PREAL, 2006, p. 6)

Quality issues also loom large in any assessment of higher education in the region. Although quality assurance has been a priority in the policy agenda since the 1990s, resources to tackle both expansion *and* quality became more plentiful in recent years as macroeconomic conditions improved in many Latin American countries.

Higher Education and Public Policy in the Last Decade

The new global economic order, trade liberalization, and a less polarized world have presented unique opportunities for economic growth for the region, which persisted through the 2008 financial crisis and until recently.[2] Awareness that increased productivity in the huge service sector and further diversification of the export base are heavily dependent upon a skilled workforce, enhanced research capacities, and technological innovation has led governments to tackle well-known deficiencies in their education systems at all levels.

To what extent and through which mechanisms is the current economic bonanza strengthening the research and advanced training capacities of top-ranking institutions in Latin America and making them more internationally competitive? How do countries manage the trade-offs between concentrating research efforts in selected institutions, enhancing quality throughout the system, and increasing access through a more diversified yet affordable system of higher education?

Comparing the performance of educational programs and institutions within and between countries in Latin America and with the rest of the world had been seriously limited by the scarcity of reliable statistical data until the 1980s. Improved educational statistics in the late 1980s and 1990s allowed a more careful diagnosis of the serious quality crisis in Latin American elementary and secondary education, reflected in issues such as grade repetition, cohort attrition, and serious achievement gaps between socioeconomic groups. The inclusion of several Latin American countries in international studies of education achievement in the 1990s and in the OECD Program for International Student Assessment since 2000 provided data showing that quantitative expansion of mass education in Latin America had failed to bring about learning outcomes comparable to those prevailing in developed countries or other emerging economies.

There are no equivalent statistics available about learning outcomes of higher education graduates. In fact, until the 1980s there was a scarcity of comparative data useful to measure educational quality of universities in Latin America. Competition for students, faculty, or resources within national systems had been traditionally limited to the private sector and based on reputation and price, since little was known about graduation rates, duration of studies, and labor market outcomes for graduates. Competitive pressures, however, have built in recent years, at least in part as a consequence of the visibility and proliferation of international and domestic ratings and rankings, however inadequately they reflect the quality of teaching and learning. The leading Latin American universities are known to do poorly in international rankings, given the weakness or low intensity of their research activities.

Universitas21, a global network of research universities, requested the University of Melbourne to rank the 48 national higher education systems with the largest scientific production in the world (Williams, De Rassenfosse, Jensen & Marginson, 2012). Four Latin American countries were included: Argentina, Brazil, Chile, and Mexico. The Latin American nations ranked very close to each other in positions ranging from the 37th (Chile) to the 43rd (Mexico), below those in North America, Western Europe, Australia, and several Eastern European and Asian countries, but above other emerging economies such as India, Indonesia, and South Africa. Although participation rates in higher education have increased in the four countries, and are already very high in Argentina and Chile, there is widespread concern about the low graduation rates, the small number of students in science and technology, the quality of teaching and learning, and the competencies and skills of graduates. Although graduate education has increased in all four countries, doctoral training is still lagging behind.

Institutional diversity within a differentiated system of higher education has been long recognized as a requirement to enhance mass access, better serve the learning needs and goals of a highly diverse student body, and preserve student selectivity within academically demanding institutions and programs. By and large, however, postsecondary enrollments in Latin America remain concentrated in university first-degree programs, which absorb more than two-thirds of the total. Although tertiary, nonuniversity institutions play a growing role in training a skilled workforce (see chapter 2 by Fanelli in this volume), public funding from central governments are concentrated in the university sector while the nonuniversity segment relies more heavily than the universities upon private funding. Mexico and Brazil have attempted in recent years to strengthen institutional segments with an explicit mission for technological education and short-cycle programs with greater accessibility attending a more diverse student body. However, generally such segments have relied heavily upon the private sector, including the for-profits, whose main limitation is their reliance on student fees.

Governments have differed in their policies of expanding the public university system to cope with increased student demands. Chile has kept a closed circle of 25 traditional universities, public and private, eligible for direct federal support. The Brazilian federal government, until recently very cautious in opening up the restricted circle of federally supported universities, has shifted gears in recent years, embarking in an expansion of federal universities and their branches, in a plan to increase access in underserved regions. In both cases, a highly differentiated sector of private providers that includes a significant for-profit segment takes the lead in absorbing demand. Argentina continues to limit the size and growth of the private system, still absorbing only some 20 percent of university undergraduates, while public university expansion proceeds under universities able to determine student intake and by Congressional authorizations to build new public universities despite the lack of an overall plan. Mexico is an example of diversification and regional decentralization of the public system, which now includes many different kinds of universities and technological schools, only a few of them with the status of autonomous, federally funded universities.

The most important step forward to increase vertical differentiation within the university sector has been taken through the growth in research funding and graduate education provided through science and technology public agencies to the most competitive universities. In recent decades, under democratic governments, agencies have given priority to funding research centers, projects, and researchers within universities rather than in autonomous government institutes. Science and technology policymaking, now conducted in closer collaboration with educational authorities and the academic community, has favored the development of research-based graduate education programs, research projects, and selected segments of the academic profession. In Brazil and Chile, and to a lesser extent in Mexico and Argentina, the link between research support and consolidation of doctoral education has been the enabling factor in identifying and supporting university programs where these functions became closer to the center of institutional life.

These and many other countries in the region have also developed in recent years more consistent efforts to increase the international involvement and competitiveness of their higher education programs, institutions, and systems, as documented in several chapters in this volume. They often require a closer collaboration between institutions—public and private—and governments, as well as more active participation of the productive sectors in the life of academic institutions, than what was possible within the traditional university model in Latin America. This is no doubt another crucial dimension of change required by higher education in the region.

NOTES

[1] The so-called Latin American model and its recent transition into a new hybrid have been discussed by a number of authors. See, for instance, Arocena and Sutz (2005) and Bernasconi (2008).

[2] The following paragraphs draw upon Balán (2012). See also Brunner and Hurtado (2011) for recent data on higher education in Ibero America.

REFERENCES

Arocena, R., & Sutz, J. (2005). Latin American universities: From an original revolution to an uncertain transition. *Higher Education, 50*, 573–592.

Balán, J. (2012). Research universities in Latin America: The challenges of growth and institutional diversity. *Social Research: An International Quarterly, 79*, 741–770.

Benavot, A., & Riddle, P. (1988). The expansion of primary education, 1870–1940: Trends and issues. *Sociology of Education, 61*, 191–210.

Benavot, A., Resnik, J., & Corrales, J. (2000). *Global educational expansion: Historical legacies and political obstacles.* Cambridge, MA: American Academy of Arts and Sciences.

Bernasconi, A. (2008). Is there a Latin American model of the university? *Comparative Education Review, 52*, 27–52.

Birdsall, N. (1996). Public spending on higher education in developing countries: Too much or too little? *Economics of Education Review, 15*, 407–419.

Birdsall, N., Ross, D., & Sabot, R. (1997). Educational growth and inequality. In N. Birdsall & F. Jaspersend (Eds.), *Pathways to growth: Comparing East Asia and Latin America.* Washington, DC: Inter-American Development Bank.

Brunner, J. J., & Hurtado, R. F. (Eds.). (2011). *Educacion superior en Iberoamerica: Informe 2011.* Santiago, Chile: Centro Interuniversitario de Desarrollo.

Frankema, E. (2009). The Expansion of Mass Education in Twentieth Century Latin America: A global comparative perspective. *Journal of Iberian and Latin American History, 27*, 359–391.

Levy, D. C. (1986). *Higher education and the state in Latin America: Private challenges to public dominance*. Chicago, IL: University of Chicago Press.

Levy, D. C. (2005). *To export progress: The golden age of university assistance in the Americas*. Bloomington: Indiana University Press.

Martínez-Fritscher, A., Musacchio, A., & Viarengo, M. (2010). *The great leap forward: The political economy of education in Brazil, 1889–1930* (Working Paper). Cambridge, MA: Harvard Business School.

Morrisson, C., & Murtin, F. (2009). *The century of education*. London, UK: London School of Economics. Retrieved from http://eprints.lse.ac.uk/28281/1/ceedp109.pdf

Newland, C. (1994). The *Estado Docente* and its expansion: Spanish American elementary education, 1900–1950. *Journal of Latin American Studies, 26*, 449–467.

Organisation for Economic Co-operation and Development (OECD). (2012). *Education at a glance 2012: OECD indicators*. Paris, France: Author. Retrieved from http://www.oecd.org/edu/eag2012.htm

PREAL. (2006). *Quantity without quality: A report card on education in Latin America 2006*. Washington, DC: Partnership for Educational Revitalization in Latin America.

Ruegg, W. (Ed.). (2004). *Universities in the nineteenth and early twentieth century*. Cambridge, UK: Cambridge University Press.

Vegas, E., & Petrow, J. (2008). *Raising student learning in Latin America : The challenge for the 21st century* . Washington, DC: The World Bank.

Williams, R., De Rassenfosse, G., Jensen, P., & Marginson, S. (2012). *U21 ranking of national higher education systems: A project sponsored by Universitas21*. Melbourne, Australia: Melbourne Institute of Applied Economic and Social Research.

Chapter One

GOVERNMENT AND UNIVERSITY AUTONOMY: THE GOVERNANCE STRUCTURE OF LATIN AMERICAN PUBLIC UNIVERSITIES

ANDRÉS BERNASCONI, PONTIFICA UNIVERSIDAD CATÓLICA DE CHILE

It is impossible to discuss university governance in the Latin American context without dealing with the notion of autonomy. The concept is not, of course, exclusive of this region of the world. In fact, a formal global definition exists, endorsed by the International Association of Universities (IAU, 1998, p. 2):

> The principle of Institutional Autonomy can be defined as the necessary degree of independence from external interference that the University requires in respect of its internal organisation and governance, the internal distribution of financial resources and the generation of income from nonpublic sources, the recruitment of its staff, the setting of the conditions of study and, finally, the freedom to conduct teaching and research.

But it seems accurate to assert that in Latin America autonomy has been the cornerstone of the system of ideas about the university as a social institution (Marsiske, 2004, pp. 161–162). Indeed, one could conceivably trace the modern history of higher education in the region since independence from Spain and Portugal in the early 19th century, and account for most if not all of its developments with respect to governance. One could then scrutinize the present state, simply by sticking to the evolution of autonomy as a feature of discourse and ideology, as an object of policy, and as an institutional practice. That is what I intend to do here, albeit in summary and in a necessarily tentative fashion, for a thorough proof of the proposition would require book-length treatment.

I first explain what university autonomy has traditionally meant within the Latin American environment, to show how some important additional prerogatives were added to the definition presented above, making it quite uniquely capacious. Next, the problem of the enduring gap between ideas and the practice of autonomy is addressed. For most of the past century, this gap has been a result of governance arrangements over higher education not living up to the exacting requirements of autonomy, as interpreted by Latin American universities. In the last two decades or so, however, it seems like the distance between rhetoric and the actual configuration of power is thinning, both as a result of changes in the policy environment and due to a redefinition of the concept of autonomy, which, albeit reluctantly, brings it closer to the international interpretation of its essential content and necessary limitations. That topic is the focus of the third and last section.

Two caveats are in order: "Latin America" is shorthand for national cases—and within-country variation of institutional experiences—that frequently resist the kind of lumping together that I will attempt here. Some overlooking of variance and special cases is the unavoidable cost of articulating the general arguments I propose. I believe that there are common threads, however, identifiable within the distinctive histories of the higher education systems of each nation, especially when it comes to ideas, and to these commonalities I bring most of my attention.

Second, my focus is on universities, leaving behind the nonuniversity sector of higher education, largely for a definitional reason: The principle of autonomy has been traditionally associated with the university as an institution, and not with the whole of higher education as a sector. Within the field of universities, my emphasis is on the autonomy and governance of public universities. There are interesting issues, too, around the autonomy and governance of private universities, which I mention in passing, but space precludes their thorough examination and recommends concentrating instead on the public university, insofar as it represents the most complex case, as well as the more comparable internationally.

The Idea of University Autonomy in Latin America

Formally, autonomy is a juridical construct that means independence from an external power, and it entails the authority of an agent to create its own rules of behavior.

This capacity to self-regulate extends to all that is required for the agent to perform its legitimate functions in pursuit of its rightful goals. Therefore, this sphere of legitimate action is at once the justification of autonomy and its limit (Abruña, Baca, & Zegarra, 2000, pp. 9–10).

It is easy to see how in a polity certain entities need to be autonomous to carry out their function: The courts, for instance, can only uphold the rule of law if they are free from interference of the other powers in their judicial mission. Or an agency responsible for organizing electoral processes and counting votes cannot be under the control of the administration, if electoral processes are to be trusted. But why should universities be autonomous?

There are two rationales for university autonomy, although both are a consequence of academic freedom. In the Continental European tradition, especially in France after the Napoleonic reforms, but also in Austria, Germany, Spain, and Scandinavia, universities have been established or refashioned since the late eighteenth century as part of the administrative structures of the nascent bureaucratic nation-states to serve their needs of education and certification. As such, universities were to exercise, by delegation from the sovereign state, the public function of awarding professional degrees. Their employees, professors included, were civil servants, and their rectors, deans, and other leaders were considered public authorities. In this model, autonomy is required by the special mission of these entities: The proper exercise of the research and teaching functions requires academic freedom, and therefore autonomy is bestowed upon the institution by the state to ensure that freedom. Accordingly, faculty are a special kind of public servants, those who are not subject, for instance, to the hierarchical authority of a superior when it comes to defining their work. Herein lies the characteristic distribution of power in the Continental model: strong at the top (the state level) and strong at the bottom (the chair-holding professors), with a weak link at the level of institutional leadership in universities (Levy, 1986, pp. 230).

In the Anglo-Saxon tradition of England, the Commonwealth countries, and even more so the United States, universities spring from civil society, so to speak, typically founded by religious groups or philanthropic interest. As such, they are not part of the civil service and do not exercise governmental powers. Unlike their Continental European peers, their degrees certify academic achievement and do not carry a professional habilitation. Their autonomy, therefore, is not a concession of the state but emanates from the general freedom of private initiative, and the freedoms of opinion and teaching in a democratic, liberal constitutional regime, rights which, by the way, governments generally lack (Abruña et al., 2000, pp. 13–18, 33).

These different sources of justification for autonomy are not homogeneous in the strength they lend to this principle of self-determination. The Continental type of autonomy is weaker, insofar as it is a concession of the state to the university, for the better service of its peculiar mission, whereas the Anglo-Saxon concept suggests that autonomy encompasses fundamental rights of individuals and organizations, which cannot be trampled by the state.

At any rate, what both notions have in common is a more or less direct backing in the freedoms of opinion, speech, and teaching. If this is so, then the primary beneficiary of this prerogative is the professor who does the thinking, speaking, and teaching. Students are also protected, insofar as they partake in the intellectual inquiry. Whence derives a first principle of governance: The protection of academic freedom at the core of the idea of autonomy requires that faculty (and students, to a lesser degree) prevail in institutional decisions of an academic nature. In other words, the decisions protected by autonomy are those adopted by scholars, because only they are holders of the rights of academic freedom. Conversely, administrative authorities, external constituents of the university, and most definitely the state, are barred by the idea of autonomy from interfering with academic matters.

But following this rationale, to protect classroom and laboratories from the interests of power and money, organizational safeguards are required as well. The protection afforded by autonomy, so the argument goes, cannot stop at the level of the individual faculty member or student: It extends to the university insofar as it is necessary to protect free inquiry and discussion. In this sense, the subject of autonomy is the university community as a whole. Whence derives a second principle of university governance, much more expansive that the first: Academic freedom involves not only academic autonomy but also normative, administrative and financial autonomy on the part of the university, necessary for the effective protection of academic freedom.

This expansive concept is the one traditionally embraced by Latin American intellectuals and universities.[1] The *Unión de Universidades de América Latina y el Caribe* (UDUAL) (Association of Universities of Latin America and the Caribbean), the oldest and largest association of universities in the region, has declared that university autonomy entails (my translation) "administrative, governance and financial independence, to ensure the fulfillment of its core functions, and protect the university from external interference" (UDUAL, 2011, p. 2). These freedoms carry for the university the capacity to create and reform its statutes and other regulations, generate its leadership, distribute its financial resources, establish its organization and the regulations for the administrative and academic personnel, and of course, maintain independence in academic matters (Abruña et al., 2000, p. 31; Nosiglia, 2004, p. 66).

So far, I have discussed autonomy at the level of the individual scholar—as defense against the meddling of forces both external to the university and against those coming from the university proprietors or sponsors—and autonomy at the level of the university as an organization. But in some parts of Latin America a claim exists to a third level of autonomy: that of the university system as a whole.[2] In practice, this autonomy prevents the government from having any higher education policy at all, save perhaps for the nonuniversity sector. This is self-governance with independence from state supervision and social oversight (Gutiérrez, 1983, pp. 2633–35). The university knows what is best for society, without needing to come under its authority. This arrangement is currently past its heyday, as will be explained later, but its vestiges can still be observed in some countries of the region, such as Bolivia, Uruguay, Costa Rica, Guatemala, Honduras, Peru, and Nicaragua. It is also a feature of the ideology of autonomy, but no longer much reflected in its practice, in Argentina, Mexico, El Salvador, and the Dominican Republic.

In other countries, such as Brazil, Chile, and Colombia, university autonomy seems not to have been understood as an exemption from democratic rule, and therefore universities were more readily deemed to be part of what in a democracy is subject to the sovereignty of the people and the governments they choose. Possibly as a result, universities have had relatively less of a problem with (democratic) governments pushing policy initiatives for higher education, especially if incremental funds are forthcoming.

In spite of these and other variations in the scope of autonomy, during the 20th century public universities in Latin American as a whole asserted, and often obtained from the state, ample room for self-determination (Bernasconi, 2007, pp. 520–524). Autonomy certainly included the usual academic freedoms to set curricula, admissions, and graduation requirements and to hire and promote faculty and staff, but it also included the prerogatives to create or close down programs, schools, or branches without governmental authorization. Administratively, universities demanded independence to define their charter and bylaws, organize their internal governance and management structures, and elect their authorities free from government involvement. They likewise demanded that financial dependence on government appropriations could not carry any directives as to how to spend the public money, and in more than a handful of countries the national constitution defined the share universities would receive of the government's annual budget.[3]

Private universities, founded in the first half of the 20th century to maintain Catholic education amid growing state secularism, or to provide for the education of the social and economic elites, and expanded in numbers toward the end of the century to provide job credentials to the masses, enjoyed a form of autonomy which in part resembled that of public universities, and in some ways differed from it. The autonomy of Catholic universities depended on the political clout of that Church in a given country, but was in any case well-guarded by the local bishops and by Rome, when needed. The situation of secular privates (and of contemporary Catholic universities, as the protection afforded by the Church has waned with the decline of its political influence, and the universities themselves have become less religious), in turn, approximates that of the institutions emerging from civil society and ideologically protected in their autonomy by the basic human freedoms of private initiative, opinion, and teaching. On the one hand, the state has often required of new private universities a period of academic supervision by a government agency or a public university, and in this sense their autonomy has been limited. On the other hand, their governance and finances have been largely outside of governmental oversight. These differences notwithstanding, the discourse of autonomy from the state is also predicated in and with respect to private universities, although with less of a political charge than in the public sector.

Brazil was a latecomer to the autonomy movement, having constitutionally proclaimed it only in 1988. This uniqueness is rooted in the history of higher education in Brazil, whose system of universities, unlike the others in the region, arose only as recently as the 1930s from stand-alone professional schools that were merged by the federal government into new federal universities throughout the country. (An exception is the state of São Paulo, which created its own state system of higher education more or less at the same time, independent of the federal government.) Throughout the foundational period, the Napoleonic model of universities as schools licensed by the state to teach and certify professional knowledge was paramount (Schwartzman, 2006). While professional training as the core function of higher education characterizes Latin American universities generally, until the late 1960s Brazil was a particularly stark case of decentralization of power to *facultades* (academic units organized around professions), with state regulation of curriculum, student admission, and graduation requirements, and universities as part of the civil service. Little use for autonomy was warranted under this scenario. Large-scale reforms were initiated in 1968, inspired by the U.S. model of disciplinary departments, elective curriculum, and research and graduate education by full-time scholars as opposed to part-time practitioners. While these reforms pointed to a new organizational and governance logic, they were enacted by a military dictatorship, and their effects on autonomy were limited until the restoration of democracy in the 1980s (Figueiredo-Cowen, 2002, pp. 475–478).

Finally, nonuniversity institutions of higher education, which represent a great variety of forms and functions throughout Latin America, have been largely excluded from the mantle of autonomy. They have not been included for these reasons: because they are not called universities, and autonomy is generally seen as an attribute of universities and not of higher education generally; their faculties do not normally fit the scholarly profile requiring academic freedom; they are more closely aligned with government policy in matters of workforce development; and, surely, their lighter political weight has resulted in more oversight and less freedom.

The Practice of Autonomy

While scattered precedents exist dating back to the late 19th century, university autonomy appeared in Latin American politics in the 1920s and 1930s (Van Aken, 1971, pp. 461). Previously, the governance of Latin American universities was quite in line with the Continental European model of limited autonomy from the state (of which the university was an agent), and most power within the university vested in faculty chairs (Figueiredo-Cowen, 2002, pp. 473). Formal proclamations of autonomy by the governments of the nations of the region, however, did not always see practical implementation in the governance patterns of national higher education systems. Often, autonomy was granted and later restricted or withdrawn, typically and most dramatically de facto during authoritarian regimes (Levy, 1986, pp. 230–233).[4]

The actual enactment of autonomy had its ebbs and flows in Latin America and significant cross-national variation, as well as differences in the status of public versus private universities. By the late 1960s, however, autonomy had gained extensive currency and had become an integral element of the Latin American notion of the university, most fully in its public version (Bernasconi, 2008, pp. 32). It included freedom from governmental steering and ample decentralization of power to *facultades*[5], with faculty, students, graduates, and administrative staff participating in the election of authorities and in membership of governing bodies at the *facultad* and university levels, an arrangement called cogovernance.[6]

While the doctrine of autonomy was intended to keep the government as far away from the university as possible, the opposite was not deemed a logical corollary. Faculty and especially students saw active participation in national politics as their right as members of the university. Much of the idea of the university as the critical "consciousness of society" ultimately translated into radical politics (Figueiredo-Cowen, 2002, pp. 473). Typically, public university members were (and continue to be[7]) more to the left of the political arc than the national mean, sometimes much more to the left. Important political parties and revolutionary movements originated or had their main recruitment base in university campuses in Chile, Peru, El Salvador, Nicaragua, and Venezuela (Levy 1986, pp. 258–259). It is no surprise, then, that rightist dictatorships made the repression of public universities a standard procedure to control dissidence.

Moreover, public universities themselves became highly politicized (Didriksson, 1994) as did private institutions following their governance model. Rectors, deans, and other officials were elected according to their affiliations in national political parties or factions, and universities were seen as much a fair target of political capture as unions, the media, and the military were. The symbiosis between university affairs and national politics was considered a natural consequence of the democratization of the university. Within this governance context, as Didriksson pointed out, Latin

American universities became notorious for their inability to sustain change in the long run. Lack of long-term goals and any possibility of meaningful movement toward a shared vision of the future, the general fragility of academic authority at the faculty level, and the electoral influence of students and administrative staff under cogovernance set the stage for the encroachment of self-perpetuating, clientelistic bureaucracies and administrative oligarchies in positions of power, sometimes alternating between rival political coalitions.

Governments shared in the responsibility for this outcome, for they rarely chose to withstand the political fallout of reforms that would be resisted by mobilized students and faculty by means of prolonged, highly disruptive, and sometimes violent strikes (Castro & Levy, 2000, pp. 80–83). The preferred method of reforming the university system was, hence, not to act upon existing public institutions but to create new ones. Venezuela did this in the 1970s and 2000s, Mexico in the 1970s and 1990s, and Argentina in the 1990s. These new public universities were often created to not resemble their more traditional peers; they were either less autonomous, in the cases of Venezuela and Mexico,[8] or organized to circumvent the *facultad* as the basic academic unit (García de Fanelli, 1998, pp. 108). But the results rarely matched the intentions. The new universities established in the 1970s resorted over time to the mores of the older ones, for instance, in Venezuela (Parra Sandoval 2004, pp. 669–670; Levy, 1986, pp. 304–305).[9]

The evolution of autonomy led to two basic types of structures for the governance of higher education systems in the region.[10] The key differentiating factor is whether higher education policy and the rules for resource allocation among universities are defined principally by the Ministry of Education or are instead prerogatives of a council of university rectors.[11] These two basic types are, of course, stylized abstractions of actual arrangements found in national legislation,[12] but with this caveat, they are nonetheless useful to connect system governance with ideas about autonomy (Bernasconi, 2011).

The most clear-cut case of self-governance by a council of university rectors is Bolivia (Brunner, 2011, pp. 375–376), where the Ministry of Education is responsible for all education with the exception of the sphere of self-determination reserved to autonomous public universities. These universities define the policies applicable to them through the normative power of the National University Congress and its executive committee. Costa Rica, Guatemala, Nicaragua, Peru, and Venezuela (although not so clearly after the 2009 reforms of the Chávez administration) are also examples of this model. This makeup reflects the extreme understanding of autonomy as explained earlier in this chapter, whereby higher education policy, as it affects public universities, is for the universities themselves to define.

The rest of the countries organize their governance of higher education mostly through the Ministry of Education or its equivalent, usually aided by a national council on education (or higher education) as a consultative or decision-making body, the composition of which is meant to represent the various educational, business, professional, government, and scientific stakeholders of higher education. A good example of this framework is the Dominican Republic's National Council for Higher Education, Science and Technology, the likes of which also exist in Colombia, Chile, and Brazil.

The internal governance of public universities, in turn, can be described in general outline as being structured the following way (Brunner, 2011, pp. 370–398): A university assembly is the top governing body,[13] consisting of a large congregation composed of all the members of the councils in the *facultades*, the rector, the deans, representatives of students, and representatives of alumni or administrative staff. This assembly is responsible for approving changes to the bylaws of the university, defining the long-term institutional plan, creating or suppressing *facultades*, and electing the rector. The norm for this and all other collegial bodies is for faculty to hold the majority of the seats.[14] Executive power is shared by the rector and a superior council integrated by the deans of *facultades* and elected members from the faculty, the students, and alumni or administrative staff. This structure is replicated at the level of the *facultad*, with a council representing the different estates and responsible for electing the dean.

Internal governance is where autonomy is defended with greatest force. It is generally understood that even if the government can steer higher education in one direction or another—and in doing so, influence the long-term trajectory of public and private universities—the internal organization of universities is off-limits to the regulatory powers of the state, all the more when universities are private. With this rationale as a background, Argentine public universities have challenged the constitutionality of 1995 legislation establishing a general framework for governance in public universities,[15] and their Bolivian peers have done likewise with respect to the obligation to participate in accreditation (Bernasconi, 1999).

If the high mark of autonomy had been achieved by the late 1960s, possibly the all-time low can be found midway through the 1980s, with dictators ruling Argentina, Brazil, Chile, Cuba, Panama, Paraguay, and Uruguay, and autonomy challenged in various degrees ranging from mild disturbances to severe interventions.[16] Since then, democracy has been established or restored in most of the region, and the relationship between governments and universities has been transformed to adapt to a new worldwide political economy of the higher education sector, one that has been variously characterized as globalization, neoliberal reform, new public management, or "academic capitalism."

Autonomy and Governance in a New Political Economy of Higher Education

Throughout the world, significant reforms of higher education governance came about as a consequence of several factors: the rekindled interest in the economic effect of science and advanced training resulting from the expectations of the knowledge economy, the refusal of governments to continue to fund all by themselves the expansion of an ever more expensive higher education, the expansion of private provision and private funding of higher education, and the allocation of strategic responsibility to university managers together with greater pressures for accountability (Bleiklie & Kogan, 2007; Christensen, 2011; Dobbins, Knill, & Vögtle, 2011).

As institutions of higher education have been required by governments beyond and within Latin America to procure funding from sources other than the state, and to become more attuned to the external demand for services like research, training, certification, consulting, and the like, the "ivory tower" concept of autonomy (which sees universities as separated from society to maintain the possibility of critical detachment) lost relevance. At the same time, a policy agenda requiring greater accountability on the part of the university sector, the rise of the model of the university integrated to the knowledge based economy, and budgetary pressures driving higher education leaders to be mindful of the notion of alternative use of public resources (Mollis, 2006, pp. 506–507) demanded of university managers to think and act more like business executives and less like public servants entrusted with the administration of a public entitlement.

Latin America has not been an exception to these trends, but starting from the singular base of its expansive notion of autonomy, it has experienced the reforms differently from Europe or Asia. Countries embodying the Continental European tradition of powerful central governments steering higher education, reforms consisted first of the devolution of decision-making power to universities and then in heightened ex post controls over the exercise of this newly reinforced autonomy (Boffo, Dubois, & Moscati, 2008; Capano, 2011; Kogan, Bauer, Bleiklie, & Henkel, 2000; Mok, 2010; Paradeise, Reale, Bleiklie, & Ferlie, 2009). In Latin America, however, only the accountability part was news, for the autonomy was already there. Since the mid-1990s, and more decidedly in the last decade, many central governments in Latin America—often prodded by the multilateral banks, or the OECD (Organisation for Economic Co-operation and Development) in the cases of Mexico and Chile—adopted a stronger role in trying to steer higher education, expecting of public institutions a more careful investment of their share of public funds, together with more intense and visible production of public goods. Additionally, governments enabled the expansion of private higher education and private funding of public higher education, introduced accreditation and other quality assurance mechanisms, and in general expanded the regulatory devices intended to keep universities accountable and aligned with the development strategies of the nation (Balán, 2006;

Bernasconi, 2008, pp. 38–41; Chiroleu, 2004; Kent, 2005, 2009; Mollis, 2006; Nosiglia, 2004, p. 87; Rama, 2005).

Mexico and Argentina offer good examples of policymaking in higher education that shapes a new understanding of the relationship between autonomy and governmental steering of higher education. Although autonomy is much cherished there, governments in the past two decades have found that they need to bring public universities in line with their modernization plans for the whole of the public sector. Governments have accordingly put forth various mechanisms, mostly in the form of incentives, but also through regulation, to stimulate a closer alignment of universities with the general reforms of the state. While *Universidad de Buenos Aires* and *Universidad Nacional Autónoma de México*, the two national (and possibly Continental) flagship universities, have been left largely undisturbed in their iconic embodiment of autonomy, governments are working instead with smaller provincial institutions, which are willing to forfeit some of their independence in exchange for additional resources, or with newly minted public universities created deliberately to serve functions or populations of relevance to the government.

UDUAL, which has been described earlier, has conceded that autonomy is changing, recognizing that nowadays it must consider the following (2011b, pp. 3–4, my translation):

- That universities need to "comply with the requirements of transparency and accountability, with the main goal of sharing the accomplishments of universities with society."

- That "processes of evaluation, accreditation and certification play an important role within a modern understanding of autonomy."

- That "relationships among universities, as well as with the business sector, need to be improved, without detriment to autonomy."

- That the "relationship with the state must be one of mutual respect, especially of autonomy, securing the financial support needed and equitable for the fulfillment of their missions."

- That "universities must consider other sources of funding, which should not be construed as granting permission to the state to abdicate from its commitment to the university and to society."

- That the "university must be open to constructive criticism, as means of achieving its validation and social legitimacy."

Over the past two decades, then, there has been greater policymaking activity in higher education on the part of governments, and public universities in the region find themselves pressed to respond to the demand for better management and greater accountability, to introduce principles and practices of professional administration and evaluation, and to measure and account for their contribution to the social good. The extent to which this pressure has ushered in fundamental change in university management, transparency, and internal governance is, however, unclear. Not only in light of the predictable delay separating intentions and implementation in every realm of organizational adaptation, but also because very little research is published on the subject of university governance and management in Latin America, we simply don't know very well what's going on.

But in terms of ideology and public pronouncements, in declarations such as UDUAL's and a myriad of others that can be found in rectors' speeches and university web pages, it seems clear that this new push toward "modernization," now in the context of globalization, is moving higher education in the region away from the discourse of extreme autonomy and vested power of internal oligarchies to greater supervision and policy direction by the governments, increased effectiveness and efficiency, more market, and more civil society. With the exception of a few highly impermeable national public flagships, and often grudgingly, Latin American universities seem to have begun to adapt their images of themselves and sense of mission to this new scenario.

How are autonomy and governance likely to evolve in the near future? System governance of higher education by the state, as I showed in the first section, is not in violation of the principle of autonomy understood as a protection of an individual's academic freedom. It may, though, limit institutional autonomy, and most definitely, system autonomy. Therefore, the effect on autonomy of greater policy activity in higher education is not immediately obvious. Governments can in fact interfere with academic autonomy if, for instance, the Ministry of Education were to select faculty members, whereas it seems harder to see a threat in the requirement put to universities that they manage their affairs more professionally.

Moreover, as more universities in the region move to really (as opposed to rhetorically) become centers for the creation, cultivation, critique, and transmission of knowledge by making their academic base more substantial, with full-time, well-trained, reasonably paid academics (as has been the case in the leading universities in Brazil, Chile, Mexico, and Colombia), self-determination tends to acquire a new meaning, closer to the original idea of academic freedom for the purposes of inquiry and farther away from the grandiose discourse of nation-building or social transformation through university militant independence.

True, becoming a hub of knowledge is indeed less of a lofty social mission than the one traditionally assigned to universities in Latin America, especially public ones, of "preparing political leaders, fostering ideological discussion, promoting social change, safeguarding tradition, and retaining and spreading the local culture" (Mollis, 2006, p. 505). But while those functions can be discharged by other social institutions, the university remains society's only institution chartered and designed to simultaneously discover, transmit, and transfer knowledge. And in Latin America, by the way, after the training of professionals, public universities have ended up serving the goal of political awareness and support of social change (which seldom went the way university ideologues wanted), a lot more than the cause of science.

In terms of the locus of power inside the universities, as leading institutions continue to replace part-time faculty active in the professions or teaching-only full-time faculty with active researchers with graduate degrees who are interested more in science than in politics, and as this new breed of academics rise to the top of their universities, the relative power of the more politicized schools (law, humanities, social sciences) would start to wane, and new centers of influence would appear in *facultades* of science, engineering, and large research centers. Such is, it seems, the trajectory of the idea of autonomy in Brazil (Schwartzman, 2006) and Chile (Bernasconi, 2010), and it is conceivable that similar paths are being trodden in the other countries of the region where research is an important component of the mission and identity of a growing part of the university sector. At any rate, for the past two decades (much earlier in Brazil) public policy in countries such as Mexico, Brazil, Argentina, and Chile has made faculty development and expansion of research capacity key goals for higher education. In a sense, governments have been asking universities to do more of what they are or should be uniquely able to do, that is, creating, acquiring, and transmitting knowledge. And this request has been backed by incremental funding not available for other purposes. Hence the paradox of governments meddling with autonomy not to subvert universities by putting them at their service, but to nudge them to better fulfill the institutional mission assigned to them.

All this academic development is taking place at the apex of the academic pecking order and therefore largely bypasses the bulk of higher education composed of teaching institutions with modest scholarship ambitions, but the modeling effect of the leading universities is not to be underestimated. Just as a the Latin American idea of autonomy gained and maintained hegemony as a set of guiding principles regardless of their actual application (and not infrequently in spite of their systematic violation), and as such colored the development of higher education in the region for nearly a century, a redefinition of functions across principal universities, a redistribution of power among their constituencies, and a new compact between governments and universities with clearer and more reliable rights and obligations for each party may over time set the bases for a new ideology for the university and for the whole of higher education in Latin America in this new century.

NOTES

[1] A recent discussion of autonomy from the point of view of university rectors can be found in UDUAL (2011a).

[2] Ana María García de Fanelli (personal communication, July 26, 2012) has suggested that this third level of autonomy may be explained as a reaction of universities in Latin America to the consequences of the various episodes of military dictatorships in the region during the 20th century.

[3] Although the financial side of autonomy is one in which the distance between discourse and practice has been widest. Even where the constitution guarantees a certain level of financing for universities, these typically claim that the government uses "creative" accounting to shrink its budgetary obligations.

[4] However, one needs to be careful about automatically associating authoritarian regimes and restrictions to autonomy. In Mexico under the PRI regime, public universities enjoyed a degree of freedom not found at that time in workers' unions and other societal institutions (Levy, 1980).

[5] I will continue to use the word *facultades* in Spanish, to distinguish the school, college, or administrative unit where programs are housed from the generic designation of scholars as a group.

[6] Cogovernance is not found in Cuba, though, where universities are part of the public administration system and have no autonomy.

[7] In the immediate advent of the Mexican presidential elections in July 2012, a symbolic election was held in Universidad Autónoma Metropolitana Xochimilco, to which students, faculty, and staff were invited to cast a vote. More than 4,000 people voted, and the leftist candidate, Andrés M. López Obrador, won 85 percent of the vote. Two weeks later, in the national elections, he got 32 percent.

[8] The new Argentine public universities are formally as autonomous as the older ones, but politically more amenable to governmental influence. In Venezuela, the Chávez government has created scores of new universities and other institutions of tertiary education based on the "Bolivarian" ideology of the regime, which have been denounced as centers for indoctrination of political cadres (García-Guadilla, 2012).

[9] Moreover, efforts backed by USAID, the Ford Foundation, and the Inter-American Bank to reform universities in the 1960s and '70s were very different in nature, scope, and results for national flagship universities, other public universities, and private universities. Many of those differences can be linked to the very different nature of autonomy and governance relationships with the governments in each case (Levy, 1995).

[10] The most up-to-date rendering of national mechanisms for higher education governance is found in Brunner (2011, 327–369).

[11] A variation of the latter model, in which universities control higher education policy, occurs in the two countries, Uruguay and Guatemala, where there exists only one public university, and this university is constitutionally responsible for overseeing higher education nationally. This is not, however, the arrangement found in other countries with only one public university, namely, El Salvador and the Dominican Republic, where higher education policy is in the hands of a ministry and not of the public university.

[12] Indeed, several combinations of actors and processes exist in practice that shape policy and resource allocation. The Ministry of Education may formally or informally discuss policy proposals with the rectors prior to their enactment, and universities and the Ministry of Education may seek to influence the budget for higher education as it is discussed in Congress.

[13] There are generally no external boards of directors in public universities in Latin America, with the exception of Chile.

[14] An exception is Bolivia, where students and faculty each have 50 percent of the stakes in electing authorities and in collegial bodies.

[15] Additionally, as Nosiglia (2004) explained, the Argentine Higher Education Act of 1995 is seen as increasing the power of the federal government via funding in detriment to university autonomy and in transferring legislative, provincial, and institutional jurisdiction to supra-university coordination bodies, which tend to standardize and homogenize practices inside institutions.

[16] The fact that even under dictatorships Latin American universities retained more autonomy than has been ever afforded to Cuban universities under the Castro regime is telling of the power of university autonomy in the region.

REFERENCES

Abruña, A., Baca, V. S., & Zegarra, A. (2000). Algunas ideas para el estudio de la autonomía universitaria en el ordenamiento peruano. *Revista de Derecho (Universidad de Piura), 1*, 9–57.

Balán, J. (2006). Reforming higher education in Latin America: Policy and practice. *Latin American Research Review, 41*(2), 228–246.

Bernasconi, A. (1999). Evaluación de la Educación Superior en América Latina: El Caballo de Troya de la Reforma. In *La Universidad Ante el Siglo XXI: Dónde estamos y hacia dónde vamos* (pp. 111–123). Caracas, Venezuela: Universidad Metropolitana.

Bernasconi, A. (2007). Constitutional prospects for the implementation of funding and governance reforms in Latin American higher education. *Journal of Education Policy, 22*(5), 509–529.

Bernasconi, A. (2008). Is there a Latin American model of the university? *Comparative Education Review, 52*(1), 27–52.

Bernasconi, A. (2010). La apoteosis del investigador y la institucionalización de la profesión académica en Chile. *ESE-Estudios sobre Educación, 19*, 139–163.

Bernasconi, A. (2011). A legal perspective on "privateness" and "publicness" in Latin American higher education. *Journal of Comparative Policy Analysis: Research and Practice, 13*(4), 351–365.

Bleiklie, I., & Kogan, M. (2007). Organization and governance of universities. *Higher Education Policy, 20*, 477–493.

Boffo, S., Dubois, P., & Moscati, R. (2008). Changes in university governance in France and in Italy. *Tertiary Education and Management, 14*(1), 13–26.

Brunner, J. J. (Ed.). (2011). *Educación superior en Iberoamérica: Informe 2011*. Santiago, Chile: CINDA y Universia.

Capano, G. (2011). Government continues to do its job: A comparative study of governance shifts in the higher education sector. *Public Administration, 89*(4), 1622–1642.

Castro, C., & Levy, D. (2000). *Myth, reality and reform: Higher education policy in Latin America*. Washington, DC: Inter-American Development Bank.

Chiroleu, A. (2004). La modernización universitaria en la agenda del gobierno argentino: Lecciones de la experiencia. *Fundamentos en Humanidades, 5*(9), 29–44.

Christensen, T. (2011). University governance reforms: Potential problems of more autonomy? *Higher Education, 62*, 503–517.

Didriksson, A. (1994). Gobierno universitario y poder. Una visión global de las formas de gobierno y la elección de autoridades en los actuales sistemas universitarios. *Perfiles Educativos, 64*. Retrieved from http://redalyc.uaemex.mx/pdf/132/13206403.pdf

Dobbins, M., Knill, C., & Vögtle, E. M. (2011). An analytical framework for the cross-country comparison of higher education governance. *Higher Education, 62*(5), 665–683.

Figueiredo-Cowen, M. (2002). Latin American universities, academic freedom and autonomy: A long term myth? *Comparative Education, 38*(4), 471–484.

García de Fanelli, A. M. (1998). *Gestión de las universidades públicas. La experiencia internacional.* Buenos Aires, Argentina: Ministerio de Cultura y Educación.

García-Guadilla, C. (2012). Polarización y tensiones en la educación superior venezolana. *Revista Iberoamericana de Educación Superior, 3*(7). Retrieved from http://ries.universia.net/index.php/ries/article/view/230/html_19

Gutiérrez, A. (1983). "El futuro de las universidades públicas. ¿Fundaciones públicas o autogestión?," *Revista de Administración Pública, 100–102*(Enero–Diciembre), 2627–2648.

International Association of Universities. (1998). *Policy statement: Academic freedom, university autonomy and social responsibility.* Retrieved from http://www.iau-aiu.net/sites/all/files/Academic_Freedom_Policy_Statement.pdf

Kent, R. (2005). La dialéctica de la esperanza y la desilusión en políticas de educación superior en México. *Revista de la Educación Superior, 34*(2), 134. Retrieved from http://www.anuies.mx/servicios/p_anuies/publicaciones/revsup/134/03.html#c

Kent, R. (2009). Capítulo 1: Una visión conceptual de los procesos de cambio en las políticas y los sistemas de educación superior. In R. Kent (Ed.), *Las políticas de educación superior en México durante la modernización. Un análisis regional* (pp. 13–38). Mexico City, Mexico: ANUIES.

Kogan, M., Bauer, M., Bleiklie, I., & Henkel, M. (2000). *Transforming higher education: A comparative study.* London, UK: Jessica Kingsley.

Levy, D. C. (1980). *University and government in Mexico: Autonomy in an authoritarian system.* New York, NY: Praeger Special Studies in Comparative Education.

Levy, D. C. (1986). *Higher education and the state in Latin America: Private challenges to public dominance.* Chicago, IL: University of Chicago Press.

Levy, D. C. (1995). *To export progress. The golden age of university assistance in the Americas.* Bloomington: Indiana University Press.

Marsiske Schulte, R. (2004). Historia de la autonomía universitaria en América Latina. *Perfiles Educativos, 26*(105–106), 160–167.

Mok, K. H. (2010). When state centralism meets neo-liberalism: Managing university governance change in Singapore and Malaysia. *Higher Education, 60*, 419–440.

Mollis, M. (2006). Latin American university transformation of the 1990s: Altered identities? In J. Forest & P. Altbach (Eds.), *International handbook of higher education. Part two: Regions and countries* (pp. 503–515). Dordrecht, The Netherlands: Springer.

Nosiglia, M. C. (2004). Transformaciones en el gobierno de la educación superior en Argentina: Los organismos de coordinación interinstitucional y su impacto en la autonomía institucional. *Fundamentos en Humanidades, 5*(9), 63–90.

Paradeise, C., Reale, E., Bleiklie, I., & Ferlie, E. (2009). *University governance: Western European perspectives.* Dordrecht, The Netherlands: Springer.

Parra Sandoval, M. C. 2004. La percepción de los académicos sobre su participación en el gobierno universitario. Estudio de caso de cuatro universidades venezolanas. *Revista Mexicana de Investigación Educativa, 9*(22), 665–691.

Rama, C. (2005). La política de educación superior en América Latina y el Caribe. *Revista de la Educación Superior, 34*(2), 134. Retrieved from http://www.anuies.mx/servicios/p_anuies/publicaciones/revsup/134/03.html

Schwartzman, S. (2006). Brazil. In J. Forest & P. Altbach (Eds.), *International handbook of higher education. Part two: Regions and countries* (pp. 503–515). Dordrecht, The Netherlands: Springer.

Van Aken, M. J. (1971). University Reform before Cordoba. *Hispanic American Historical Review, 51*(3), 447–462.

Unión de Universidades de América Latina y el Caribe. (2011a). *Universidades 49*(Abril–Junio). Retrieved from http://www.udual.org/CIDU/Revista/49/Revista49.pdf

Unión de Universidades de América Latina y el Caribe. (2011b). *Conclusiones del Foro La autonomía universitaria hoy: Experiencias y desafíos en América Latina*. Retrieved from http://www.udual.udg.mx/conclusiones/FORO%20AU%20UNIV%202011%20CONCLUSIONES.pdf

Chapter Two

TRAINING THE 21ST CENTURY KNOWLEDGE WORKERS: HIGHER EDUCATION AND WORKFORCE DEVELOPMENT IN LATIN AMERICA

ANA GARCÍA DE FANELLI, CENTRO DE ESTUDIOS DE ESTADO Y SOCIEDAD-CONICET, ARGENTINA

A common characteristic of Latin American economies is that they have long stagnated in the middle-income category. This is particularly true in Argentina, Brazil, Chile, Mexico, and Venezuela, the largest economies in the region, which together represent 78 percent of its GDP (ECLAC [Economic Commission for Latin America and the Caribbean], 2012). Two additional features that these countries share are (1) they averaged low economic growth rates in the second half of the 20th century, especially compared to the growth rates of the four Asian Tigers (Hong Kong, Singapore, South Korea, and Taiwan); and (2) they have all experienced periods of growth accelerations and crises, suggesting that the obstacles to economic development have more to do with sustaining growth than with igniting it. In the 2000s, regional growth accelerated for the first time since the debt crisis the 1980s, while poverty levels and income distribution improved. In light of the experience of recent decades, it is not surprising that the recent acceleration in growth has been perceived as a window of opportunity for the region. At the same time, many analysts have expressed concern about the need to reinforce investment in human and institutional capital to ensure growth sustainability and escape the "middle-income trap."

Two points are key in this regard. The first is that growth resumption—particularly in natural resource–rich South America—has been closely related to the positive evolution of the terms of trade. Hence, to avoid the so-called natural resource curse, it is crucial to generate conditions that are conducive to the accumulation of human capital and technological progress (Sinnott, Nash, & de la Torre, 2010). The second is that the region is going through a demographic bonus stage in which both labor force participation and savings rates are high. This demographic dividend, however, can become a liability if savings are wasted and high-quality jobs are not created. The bonus is followed by the aging stage, during which there will be mounting pressure on government budgets because of the rising cost of social security and health care. If Latin America becomes old before it can become rich, escaping the middle-income trap will be harder. To create high-quality jobs during the dividend stage it is critical to invest in human capital and to foster structural changes that are friendly to innovation. These conditions will help make growth not only sustainable, but also inclusive.

Higher education is crucial to preparing and certifying the competent human capital necessary to face this challenge. It is also responsible for imparting high-level technical skills and producing new knowledge and technological innovation. This chapter will analyze some indicators of advanced human capital in Latin America, along with employment outcomes and available information about the labor market insertion of tertiary graduates.

Advanced Human Capital in Latin America

In knowledge societies, higher education is one of the most important ways to invest in human capital. It contributes to economic and human development through teaching the skills, competencies, and knowledge necessary to create a pool of scientists, top-level officials, high-level professionals, and technicians. Moreover, higher education makes it possible to officially certify the level of knowledge and competencies required to perform scientific, professional, and technical jobs in the labor market, while also providing opportunities to update knowledge and continuous training through graduate programs and courses. Moreover, a tertiary-educated workforce is particularly important for innovation and the adoption of new technologies.

The population that completed tertiary studies increased dramatically worldwide between 1950 and 2010. In Latin America, the proportion of the total population ages 15 and over that completed their tertiary studies grew 12-fold in this period.

Although this was a huge jump in the stock of human capital, it still lags significantly behind developed countries (see Table 2.1).

TABLE 2.1: PROPORTION OF THE TOTAL POPULATION AGED 15 AND OVER THAT ATTAINED TERTIARY LEVEL COMPLETED BY REGION OF THE WORLD, 1950 AND 2010

Region	1950	2010
World	1.1	6.7
Advanced	2.8	14.5
Developing	0.5	5.1
Developing by Region:		
Middle East and North Africa	0.5	6.0
Sub-Sahara Africa	0.1	0.9
Latin America and the Caribbean	0.6	7.1
East Asia and the Pacific	0.2	5.8
South Asia	0.3	3.0
Europe and Central Asia	1.5	9.9

Source: Barro & Lee (2010).

In particular, the average length of education in Latin America increased considerably during the 1990s and the first decade of the 2000s, although this indicator did not change at the same pace in all parts of the region. The average length of schooling for adults aged 25–65 surpassed nine years in only a few countries. Argentina and Chile have the highest average length of education in Latin America (11 years), while adults in Guatemala, Honduras, and Nicaragua average less than six years of education. Moreover, a large gap—6.5 years—exists between the average number of years of education for adults in the top quintile versus those in the bottom quintile (Cruces, Garcia Domenech, & Gasparini, 2011). [1]

Although more than 16 percent of the adult population (25–64 years old) holds tertiary degrees in certain Latin American countries (LACs) such as Chile, Argentina, and Mexico, they still lag far behind many developed countries (see Figure 2.1).

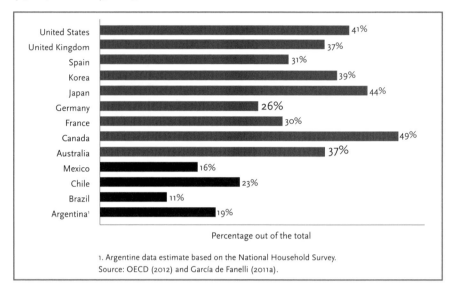

1. Argentine data estimate based on the National Household Survey.
Source: OECD (2012) and García de Fanelli (2011a).

Even though tertiary attainment levels in Latin America have risen considerably over the past 50 years, the issue of improving the preparedness of secondary-level graduates applying to higher education institutions is still pending. The results of the Program for International Student Assessment (PISA), a global student achievement test that assesses the skills of 15-year-olds in math, reading, and science, reveal the challenges that LACs must face if they wish to participate in the knowledge society.[2] Many LACs have sought to improve the preparedness of secondary graduates in order to achieve better quality in higher education. Some countries, like Brazil and Chile, have applied selective admissions policies to choose the best secondary graduates to enter the public-funded university sector. But the excess demand that results from these policies is being absorbed by less selective higher education institutions, the majority of which belong to the private sector. This implies that even in these countries, a significant proportion of tertiary graduates have not had the opportunity to acquire appropriate knowledge and skills at the secondary level. Moreover, these students have to study in higher education institutions with poor teaching and research resources. Their likelihood of choosing careers in science and technology is strongly influenced by the quality of their secondary-level training in mathematics and sciences.

Ganimian and Solano Rocha (2011) presented the alarming results of PISA for Latin America. They showed that countries in the region ranked in the bottom third in all subjects tested. Chile outperformed the rest of the region in reading and science, but matched the others in math. Panama and Peru recorded the worst performance in all subjects. The authors also stated that a large percentage of the students did not reach minimum skill levels (30–80 percent performed at the lowest levels according to the country and subject), and that less than 3 percent of students in all countries in the region registered among the top performers. Finally, they pointed out that these LACs did poorly when compared to others with similar per capita income, even when taking into account their levels of investment in education. On the positive side, Ganimian and Solano Rocha mentioned that some LACs improved their performance in relation to previous tests.[3]

Another important dimension to consider is the flow of graduates according to the broad field of study. Unfortunately, available data do not distinguish between university graduates (four to six years of coursework) and other tertiary graduates (two to three years of coursework). We will thus have to treat the following conclusions as tentative.

Across LACs, the distribution of graduates by field of study shows that between one-third and one-half studied the social sciences (see Table 2.2). This pattern is similar to some developed countries included in this table, with the exception of Finland, South Korea, and Germany, which show less than one-quarter graduating in social science fields. The significance of the social sciences among tertiary graduates is consistent with the increasing proportion of employment provided by jobs in the service sector. In 2010, the proportion of the total population employed in the service sector in LACs was lowest in Bolivia (46.4 percent) and highest in Argentina (75.5 percent) (ECLAC, 2012).[4]

At the other extreme, apart from such developed countries as Australia, France, Germany, and the United Kingdom, the proportion of graduates in the science fields is quite low, less than 9 percent of the total.

TABLE 2.2: GRADUATES BY BROAD FIELD OF EDUCATION AND GENDER IN TERTIARY EDUCATION. SELECTED LATIN AMERICAN AND ADVANCED COUNTRIES, 2009 (%)

COUNTRY	Edu, Hum, Arts[1]		Social Sciences[2]		Science[3]		Eng, Man, Cons[4]		Agriculture[5]		Health-Welfare[6]		Services[7]		UN[8]	Total	Female
	Total	Female	Total	Female	Total	Female	Total	Female	Total	Female	Total	Female	Total	Female			
Latin American countries																	
Argentina	28	79	35	62	7	54	7	35	3	42	16	73	4	29		100	64
Brazil	26	77	38	55	7	35	6	28	2	39	14	75	2	65	5	100	61
Chile	23	72	30	56	6	24	15	20	3	42	18	77	6	47		100	55
Colombia	15	62	52	54	2	51	22	36	1	43	8	72				100	53
Mexico	18	69	42	59	9	43	16	28	2	35	9	64	3	60		100	54
Panama	30	76	38	71	5	51	15	37	1	48	7	75	5	59		100	66
Uruguay	21	82	36	66	7	49	7	40	5	31	23	75	3	19		100	66
Advanced countries																	
Australia	19	68	44	54	10	36	8	24	1	49	15	77	3	53		100	56
Republic of Korea	26	70	21	46	8	37	24	24	1	40	14	71	6	46		100	50
Finland	21	77	24	68	8	46	21	23	2	59	20	86	6	76		100	63
France	12	71	41	63	11	36	16	23	1	38	15	73	4	47		100	55
Germany	26	74	22	53	12	44	12	18	2	40	22	78	3	54	1	100	58
Netherlands	23	71	37	52	6	21	8	19	1	52	19	75	5	53	1	100	57
Spain	22	74	26	63	9	35	16	28	2	47	16	77	8	54	1	100	58
United Kingdom	27	67	31	55	13	38	9	21	1	62	18	78	1	59	1	100	57
United States	23	68	38	56	8	41	7	19	1	47	15	82	7	55		100	58

Note on UNESCO classification by fields of education:

1. Education, humanities, and arts
2. Social sciences: social and behavioral science, journalism and information, business and administration, and laws
3. Science: life sciences, physical sciences, mathematics and statistics, and computing
4. Engineering, manufacturing, and construction: engineering and engineering trades, manufacturing and processing, and architecture and building
5. Agriculture: agriculture, forestry and fishery, and veterinary
6. Health and welfare: health and social services
7. Personal services: transport services and environmental protection
8. Not known or unspecified

Source: Calculation based on UIS (2012a).

With respect to the training of engineers, Table 2.2 shows that the proportion of Latin American tertiary graduates in the broader fields of engineering, manufacturing, and construction varies by country. This may be due to a different mix of university and tertiary nonuniversity programs in each case. Argentina, Brazil, and Uruguay show a smaller proportion of graduates in these fields compared to Chile, Colombia, Mexico, and Panama. In Chile and Colombia, for example, the proportion of graduates in relatively short tertiary nonuniversity technical programs is significant.

Argentina and Brazil produce one undergraduate engineer for every 6,700 and 6,000 inhabitants, respectively, while Mexico and Chile produce one in 4,500. This contrasts with China, where the rate is one in 2,000, and Germany and France, where it is one in 2,300 (ME [Ministerio de Educación de la Argentina], 2012).

In terms of female participation, women are overrepresented among tertiary graduates, especially in the fields of education, the humanities, arts, health and welfare, and, to a lesser extent, the social sciences. Despite their high rates of participation in the graduate population, women are generally underrepresented among graduates in the sciences, engineering, manufacturing, and construction (see Table 2.2).

It is important to pay attention not only to the flow of graduates but also to the distribution of professionals in certain fields in each country. Regrettably, data that would enable comparisons between the stock of advanced human capital in different LACs are not available. Limited information exists on the physician population, for example. The number of inhabitants per physician is remarkably low in Argentina (327), Cuba (155), and Uruguay (235). In contrast, the number of inhabitants per physician amounts to 5,235 in Guatemala, 2,330 in Nicaragua, and more than 1,000 in Bolivia, the Dominican Republic, Guyana, and Paraguay (ECLAC, 2012).

Tertiary Graduates and the Labor Market

This section will analyze the relationship between tertiary graduates and the labor market by focusing on three quantitative labor and income indicators: the unemployment rate by level of education, the quality of jobs measured by the percentage of the labor force in the informal sector, and the rate of return to education. In addition, qualitative information produced by each Ibero-American country for the book *Educación Superior en Iberoamérica: Informe 2011* (Brunner & Ferrada Hurtado, 2011) will be analyzed in order to determine how much is known about this subject. Finally, three case studies on the tertiary nonuniversity sector in Brazil, Colombia, and Mexico will highlight the role of these short-term technical and technological programs for economic and social development.

	Incomplete primary	Complete primary	Incomplete lower secondary	Incomplete secondary school	Complete secondary school	Incomplete tertiary	Complete tertiary	Total
Argentina	7.6	6.7	7.4	6.3	6.9	6.1	2.3	6.0
Bolivia	1.9	1.5	0.7	2.7	2.4	4.9	4.7	2.6
Brazil	3.7	3.3	4.8	5.4	5.0	3.1	2.6	4.2
Chile	6.0	4.2	5.5	6.0	5.1	4.7	2.5	5.0
Colombia	6.5	7.1	8.5	9.0	16.3	9.4	6.3	7.7
Costa Rica	4.7	3.0	3.2	3.5	1.9	2.4	0.6	2.8
Dominican Republic	8.7	11.1	10.9	12.5	12.4	9.2	4.4	10.1
Ecuador	2.6	2.7	3.2	2.8	4.9	4.7	3.4	3.4
El Salvador	5.1	4.2	5.7	5.6	4.0	4.5	3.6	4.8
Guatemala	0.8	0.6	1.8	0.0	2.2	2.6	1.1	1.1
Honduras	1.5	1.7	2.3	3.1	2.0	1.8	1.6	1.7
Mexico	2.7	2.6	2.7	2.0	2.7	1.7	2.6	2.5
Panama	1.3	2.5	3.7	3.2	2.9	4.8	2.2	2.9
Paraguay	2.8	3.4	5.0	4.3	2.7	2.0	0.0	3.2
Peru	0.8	0.7	1.8	3.3	3.2	3.1	3.8	2.2
Uruguay	5.7	5.0	5.8	4.6	3.5	3.2	1.9	4.5
Venezuela	4.5	4.8	4.6	4.3	4.2	5.6	3.7	4.5

Source: ECLAC (2011)

Labor and Income Indicators

In Latin America, people with some college education are more likely to be employed and to obtain high-quality jobs. With respect to the first issue, within a context of low unemployment rates across LACs during the 2005–10 period, tertiary graduates generally show lower unemployment rates compared to those with secondary degrees (see Table 2.3). The main exceptions are countries like Bolivia, where more than half of the employed population works in the informal sector.

As for the quality of the jobs, the probability of employment in informal jobs is significantly lower among workers with higher education throughout Latin America (see Table 2.4).

TABLE 2.4: PROPORTION OF EMPLOYED POPULATION AGE 15 AND OVER WORKING IN THE INFORMAL SECTOR OUT OF THE TOTAL AND OUT OF THE POPULATION WITH TERTIARY LEVEL IN LAC AROUND 2007

Country	Tertiary level		
	Total	Incomplete tertiary	Complete tertiary
Argentina	39.8	27.2	13.7
Bolivia	71.2	31.7	14.4
Brazil	36.5	11.8	10.2
Chile	31.5	17.0	5.2
Colombia	63.7	37.3	16.9
Costa Rica	40.1	16.1	7.4
Dominican Republic	55.7	18.8	12.5
Ecuador	63.0	32.9	19.2
El Salvador	59.4	21.1	14.3
Guatemala	54.9	18.9	6.5
Honduras	57.8	20.3	10.8
Mexico	50.4	23.3	14.1
Nicaragua	66.1	37.3	17.3
Panama	47.0	22.6	8.7
Paraguay	65.9	21.2	11.0
Peru	68.3	46.0	21.3
Uruguay	41.3	16.2	8.3
Venezuela	48.9	29.2	11.2

Source: ECLAC (2011)

Finally, the private rate of return to higher education is high in some LACs, averaging 15 percent yearly for postsecondary education (ECLAC, 2011). Nonetheless, the rate differs widely among countries and depends on the supply of college graduates, with a minimum of 8.3 percent in the case of Argentina and a maximum of 26 percent in Brazil (see Figure 2.2).

FIGURE 2.2: INTERNAL RATES OF RETURN TO EDUCATION IN LATIN AMERICAN COUNTRIES AROUND 2008 (%)

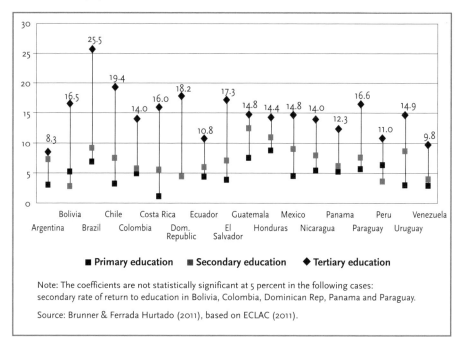

Note: The coefficients are not statistically significant at 5 percent in the following cases: secondary rate of return to education in Bolivia, Colombia, Dominican Rep, Panama and Paraguay.

Source: Brunner & Ferrada Hurtado (2011), based on ECLAC (2011).

In terms of wage premium, in 2009 the average wages of a male worker with a college education were 49 percent higher than the wages of a male worker with only a secondary education. They were 82 percent higher in Brazil, 89 percent higher in Chile, and reached an extreme of 104 percent higher in Costa Rica (SEDLAC [Socio-Economic Database for Latin America and the Caribbean], 2011).[5]

Although women's rates of return tend to be higher, their income levels are consistently lower than men's. The gender wage gap among workers with more than 13 years of education is high in countries like Brazil, where women earned on average 64.2 percent of men's wages in 2009. The majority of other LACs show a gender wage ratio ranging from 70 to 80 percent (ECLAC, 2011).

Information on Higher Education Employment in Latin America

Public officials and higher education experts often draw attention to the skill and competency mismatches between the education provided at Latin American higher education institutions and skills that are relevant at work. A similar contrast is drawn between the concentration of graduates in certain fields of study and the scarcity of graduates with training that prepares them for high-demand professions. Though these discrepancies may exist, empirical evidence related to this matter in Latin America is incomplete in terms of fields of study, countries, economic sectors, and periods of time.

According to Teichler (2009, p. 8), although educational systems are often expected to adapt to the "requirements" of the employment system, close linkages between educational curricula and career success are difficult to achieve. Teichler stressed that available research indicated that it is especially difficult to identify the educational competencies necessary to succeed in highly skilled occupational areas. Individuals are not merely expected to take over tasks that could be anticipated and taught in advance, but also to question existing rules, innovate, and cope with indeterminate work tasks. Because of the number of years needed to revise and implement new curricula, there is also an unavoidable time gap between the identification of new job assignments and the "production" of graduates equipped with the relevant competencies.

Given the difficulties of determining the needs of the labor market or trying to make long-term forecasts for human capital requirements,[6] the best solution may simply be to increase access to information about how graduates of the main higher education programs fare in terms of wages and employability. Alternatively, public policies can promote university policies geared to producing innovative curricula and combining general education with work experience and graduate follow-up studies.[7] In particular, follow-up studies can clarify the match or mismatch among the knowledge, skills, and competencies acquired in higher education and those demanded by the graduates' work.

In most LACs, neither governments nor institutions have collected sufficient information on the employment of college graduates. The few governmental initiatives involve "labor observatories." These observatories collect information on levels of employability, average wages by program during the first and subsequent years, wage dispersion for professionals and technicians, and the degree of job satisfaction, among others. One example is the website Futuro Laboral, created by Chile's Ministry of Education in 2003 (MINEDUC, 2012). This initiative collects information on employment and wage background from a selection of graduates of the most popular professional and technical programs. The results are published by program with information about monthly gross income, monthly income dispersion, employability a year after graduation, the number of graduates, new enrollment, and tuition and fees. According to the government, this initiative will help to solve existing market failures owing to the lack of information available to students when choosing their course. It is based on the idea that making labor and income indicators accessible will improve the articulation between program curricula and labor market requirements (Zapata et al., 2011). A similar initiative is the "Educación Superior en Colombia-Informe Nacional," which encourages the collection of information on higher education graduates and data on labor integration and new graduates' average wages (Orozco Silva, Castillo Gómez, & Varelo, 2011).

As an example of the kind of analysis that can be carried out with this type of information, Table 2.5 shows Chile's employability indicator and the average wage at the entry level (within the first year after graduation) and five years later for selected academic fields. Wages are expressed as a percentage of the average salary of graduates in chemistry. The data show that at the entry level and five years later, only graduates in the humanities (arts and literature) and education earn less than chemistry graduates. The top wage earners are physicians, followed by industrial civil engineers and metal-mechanical engineers. Moreover, the wage gap between these graduates and those in chemistry widens after five years. Also, the average entry-level wage of lawyers is 71 percent higher than chemistry graduates. There are also substantial differences in the employability indicator. The percentage of graduates employed after the first year of graduation ranged from 49 percent in the arts to over 90 percent in medicine and engineering programs. In terms of wage premium and employability, the most fitting programs are medicine, industrial civil engineering, and metal-mechanical engineering. This table clearly shows that the demand for industrial civil engineers, metal-mechanical engineers, physicians, and lawyers is higher than for chemistry graduates or graduates of other programs in the table.

TABLE 2.5: CHILE: AVERAGE WAGE IN SELECTED FIELDS IN TERMS OF PERCENT VARIATION FROM THE AVERAGE SALARY IN CHEMISTRY IN OCTOBER 2011; EMPLOYABILITY WITHIN FIRST YEAR AFTER GRADUATION IN SELECTED UNIVERSITY PROGRAMS

University programs	Mean wage		Employability[1]
	1st year	5th year	
Accountant – Auditor	38.9	28.5	85.9
Business Administration	8.9	1.6	79.8
Law	71.3	112.5	79.4
Arts	–11.0	–24.3	48.6
Pedagogy in Basic Education	–27.1	–30.4	80.0
Literature	–22.7	–20.0	64.5
Chemistry	0.0	0.0	67.8
Psychology	2.6	7.9	78.9
Medicine	130.4	174.2	93.0
Industrial Civil Engineering	103.9	141.4	93.7
Metal mechanical Engineering	100.9	148.1	94.8
Agronomy	16.6	34.3	78.6
1. Percentage of employability within first year of graduation.			

Source: Calculation based on MINEDUC (2012).

While governments like Chile and Colombia provide some information about the labor and income status of their higher education graduates, universities have begun to conduct follow-up surveys of alumni in order to supply data for external evaluators and course accreditation. In Argentina, special software has been developed for this purpose. Two surveys must be given to the graduate population. The first must be conducted with new graduates, and the second must be conducted one year later. A postgraduation survey after five years is now being considered. Additionally, some national universities have created job bank websites and internships to facilitate the transition from the university to the labor market (García de Fanelli, 2011a). Nonetheless, information collected by Latin American public and private universities on graduate follow-ups has not been systematized and is not generally used to update and improve the quality and relevance of the curricula. Some universities, especially private ones, use part of this information as a kind of promotion to attract students.

Qualitative information collected in Argentina and Brazil highlight the presence of unmet labor demands in engineering and computer sciences. In Argentina, executives in the country's leading technology companies underscore the lack of engineers in specialties including computer sciences, electronics, and engineering fields such as electrical, civil, chemical, petroleum, and mining engineering (García de Fanelli,

2011a). In Brazil, the most requested jobs requiring higher education are found in information technology, mining, petrochemistry, energy, civil construction, medicine, and labor security. Analyzing possible future professions through 2020, professors at the University of São Paulo conducted research that indicates that in Brazil, career fields with greater demand for professionals will be those related to quality of life and the aging of the population, such as biotechnology, nanotechnology applied to medicine, recreation, and tourism, as well as career fields linked to concerns about the environment and global integration, such as sustainability and international relations (Leal Lobo, 2011).

As for governmental concerns over the low number of graduates in the sciences, the main potential employers of scientists are public and private organizations devoted to research and development (R&D). As such, increasing the proportion of science graduates basically depends on investment in R&D. A common international indicator that reflects a country's level of innovation activities in relative terms is the "R&D intensity," which is based on gross domestic expenditure on R&D as a percentage of the GDP. The majority of developed countries spent more than 2 percent of their GDP on R&D in 2009. Among LACs, in contrast, Argentina and Cuba spent between 0.5 and 0.7 percent. Brazil reported the highest level of intensity (1.1 percent), but Colombia, Chile, and Mexico spent less than 0.4 percent of their GDP on R&D (UIS [UNESCO Institute of Statistics], 2012b). In order to prevent a brain drain and to encourage students to apply to science programs, public policies should focus on strengthening science and technology institutions and PhD and postdoctoral programs, as well as on improving the incentive structure (average wages and employability) for faculty and researchers.

In sum, studies carried out mainly by researchers specializing in labor issues and using data from national household surveys highlight the profitability of investment in higher education. Nonetheless, precise data regarding different professional scenarios are scarce, which makes it difficult for students to make vocational decisions and for governments to design public policy. Developing a system to collect this information, as well as publicly disseminating the results of surveys administered to graduates, would be useful both for students and for educators revising syllabi. The effects would also be felt in other institutional and public strategies that aim to optimize the relationship between higher education and the labor market.

The Nonuniversity Higher Education Sector and the Labor Market

The Latin American nonuniversity higher education tier includes not only institutions like teacher-training institutes and technical and semiprofessional schools but also a wide range of short-term courses (generally, two or three years long) that universities offer as intermediate or final degrees. In consequence, two organizational types coexist in the same system: the binary system, which is composed of a group of universities and other nonuniversity higher education institutions whose courses are not articulated with one another, and the integrated system, where universities themselves provide both degrees.

Higher education enrollment in Latin America is concentrated in undergraduate programs, especially professional ones. Argentina, Chile, Colombia, Peru, and Venezuela have over 25 percent of the enrollment in the nonuniversity higher education programs (Brunner & Ferrada Hurtado, 2011).

Low-income students find these programs more attractive than undergraduate programs. First, in most LACs the best public and private universities select their students through entrance exams, and in some cases, only a limited number of openings are available per course (for example, in Chile, Brazil, Bolivia, and Peru). In general, secondary school alumni from low socioeconomic backgrounds that aspire to enroll in higher education lack the opportunity to attend high-quality public or private secondary schools. Moreover, they are usually among the first generation in their family to attend university. This implies unequal opportunities to access higher education compared to students from more advantaged backgrounds. Second, nonuniversity higher education institutions are better distributed regionally, which allows students to avoid the high costs of having to move to large cities where the majority of the universities are located. Finally, these programs are attractive because they are short (reducing the opportunity cost for students and their families derived from investing in higher education), and they have a more vocational or technical orientation (García de Fanelli & Jacinto, 2011).

Employment information on nonuniversity tertiary graduates in Latin America is even more limited than that which exists for university graduates. A case study of Brazil, Colombia, and Mexico, sponsored by the International Institute for Educational Planning (IIEP-UNESCO) Paris, allows us to examine this underexplored area (García de Fanelli, 2011b). These national reports show that different factors have led to the most recent expansion in nonuniversity programs. First, it was a consequence of academic drift and professionalization of training for certain occupations, such as tour guide, fashion designer, cook, or hotel administrator—employees in these fields had previously received training at unofficial vocational institutions and on the job. Second, the expansion in nonuniversity programs can also be traced to the actions of professional corporations and regulatory agencies (mainly in healthcare) that put mechanisms in place to control the education levels of workers hoping to access the labor market. Finally, it has been a response to a demand for workers trained in information and communication technology.

A special report sponsored by the MINEDUC (Meller, Lara, & Valdés, 2009) highlighted that in Chile, the demand for technical tertiary graduates increased between 2001 and 2006, in particular in the education fields of business and administration. At the same time, the demand decreased for gastronomy and system analysts.[8]

Given the novelty of these postsecondary programs, employers in some countries do not yet clearly distinguish between technicians trained at the secondary level and those at the tertiary level. In Brazil, for example, this confusion is aggravated by the use of equal designation to refer to programs offered at different educational levels (secondary, postsecondary) (Barato, 2010). This contrasts with Colombia, where employers are already beginning to differentiate between technicians and higher education technologists (Turbay, 2010).

With respect to income levels, the average salary of nonuniversity tertiary graduates in Brazil, Colombia, and Mexico tends to be lower than those obtained by higher education graduates. This can partly be explained by the lower investment that these students make in terms of years of study. University courses usually take at least twice as long as tertiary programs (García de Fanelli, 2011b). In spite of having a lower average income in comparison to university professionals, nonuniversity tertiary graduates interviewed in the Colombian case study were satisfied with their salary and training. Moreover, in Colombia, 66.4 percent of the professional technicians and 73.6 percent of the technologists worked in the formal sector, compared with 76.7 percent of the university graduates. For men, attaining a college degree means a starting salary that can be 52 percent higher than technical graduates and 34 higher than technologists (Graduados Colombia Observatorio Laboral, 2011a).[9]

As far as employers are concerned, nonuniversity graduates are positively valued. From the survey conducted among Brazilian employers, one can conclude that more employers predict a higher increase in the demand for technologists than those who augur a similar scenario for engineers (García de Fanelli, 2011b).

Conclusions

The huge increase in advanced human capital in LACs over recent decades is positive. However, the gap between LACs and developed countries still persists, and there is a wide variation in the number of years for the adult population in the LACs. Argentina and Chile have the most educated adult population in the region, while Guatemala, Honduras, and Nicaragua present the least educated. Aggregate data on the distribution of graduates by fields of knowledge also reveal a concentration in the social sciences and humanities and a low proportion in the field of science.

Neither governments nor higher education institutions produce clear evidence of the quality and relevance of this human capital expansion. Even though many LACs implement procedures for quality assessment and the accreditation of institutions and programs, information on the quality of graduates in terms of skills and knowledge corresponding to a fitting performance in the labor market is generally scarce. Nor is there evidence of the lack of matching between graduates of higher education institutions in Latin America and the requirements of the economic and social growth of these countries. Information is available only in some specific cases and in particular economic situations.

Global indicators, such as employability and income differentials by level of education in LACs, show that tertiary graduates generally have lower unemployment rates than secondary graduates, work mainly in the formal sector of the economy, and earn substantially more than secondary graduates typically earn in all countries for which data exist. However, this information, based on national household surveys, provides limited information on the relevance of some higher education programs. The level of aggregation of the data makes it difficult to analyze clearly the relative situation of different degrees and compare university and nonuniversity tertiary graduates in the labor market. In this regard, the information provided by the labor observatories in Chile and Colombia is more suitable for analyzing the relative importance of different professions for the economy and society. It can also serve to guide students on employment opportunities and income in the labor market.

In recent years, universities have developed strategies to link students' training and the labor market via, for example, internship programs and case study methods. They have also begun to conduct follow-ups of graduates. Ideally, these experiences will lead to universities' designing policies aimed at updating and improving the quality and relevance of the curricula.

Finally, the need to foster the development of high-tech fields to guarantee growth sustainability and escape the "middle-income trap" should be approached not only from the point of view of the number of graduates in science and technology but especially considering the financial and institutional resources available to these graduates. The weakness of science and technology agencies and the limited and volatile regional funds allocated to R&D encourage the brain drain to developed countries where these fields are already thriving.

NOTES

[1] The countries included in Cruces et al.'s (2011) report are Argentina, Bolivia, Brazil, Chile, Colombia, Costa Rica, Dominican Republic, Ecuador, El Salvador, Guatemala, Honduras, Mexico, Nicaragua, Panama, Paraguay, Peru, Uruguay, and Venezuela.

[2] The Latin American countries that participated in the 2009 PISA were Argentina, Brazil, Chile, Colombia, Mexico, Panama, Peru, Venezuela, and Uruguay.

[3] According to Aedo & Walke (2012), progress in test scores compared to previous years can be attributed to improvements in grade age correspondence (placing more 15-year-olds in suitable classes corresponding to their age group), but the average learning achievement of those who were already in the right grade showed little improvement.

[4] The U.S. Department of Labor's employment projections also show that many different specialties in management and administration are among the occupations that will need to grow by more than 20 percent between 2010 and 2020 (U.S. Department of Labor, 2012).

[5] During the first decade of the 2000s, the wage premium for tertiary and secondary education declined with respect to the 1990s, contributing to the reduction in income inequality and poverty (Aedo & Walke, 2012). Preliminary studies on this issue show that different factors explain this phenomenon, such as the rising supply of educated workers, the effect of changes in terms of trade through the structure of production and relative labor demand for skills, and the scope of redistributive policies and minimum wages (Aedo & Walke, 2012; Gasparini et al., 2011).

[6] In a global economy, and particularly in the volatile Latin American macroeconomic contexts, it is difficult to make long-term human capital demand forecasts.

[7] See Scheele & Brunner (2009) for a review of the international literature on the main strategies developed by the European Community and higher education institutions to increase the employability of graduates.

[8] For more information about professional technical education in Chile, including the programs with higher average earnings and the dispersion of income at this level of education vis-à-vis university programs, see Meller & Brunner (2009).

[9] At the technical training level, a recent male graduate in 2008 obtained an average starting salary of Colombian $981,252 and a female graduate earned $825,557. With technology training, the men received an average salary of Colombian $1,110,299 and $957,194 for women (Graduados Colombia Observatorio Laboral, 2011b).

REFERENCES

Aedo, C., & Walke, I. (2012). *Skills for the 21st century in Latin America and the Caribbean.* Washington DC: World Bank.

Barato, J. (2010). *Educación técnica y tecnológica Pos-secundaria: Tendencias, enfoque y desafíos en Brasil* (report). Paris, France: IIPE-UNESCO.

Barro, R., & Lee, J. (2010). *A new data set of educational attainment in the world, 1950–2010* (Working Paper No. 15902). Cambridge, MA: NBER.

Brunner, J. J., & Ferrada Hurtado, R. (Eds.). (2011). *Educación superior en Iberoamérica: Informe 2011.* Santiago, Chile: CINDA-UNIVERSIA.

Cruces, G., Garcia Domenech, C., & Gasparini, L. (2011). *Inequality in education: evidence for Latin America* (Report). CEDLAS UNLP and UNUWIDER. Retrieved from http://www.wider.unu.edu/stc/repec/pdfs/wp2011/wp2011-093.pdf

ECLAC. (2011). *Social panorama of Latin American 2010.* Santiago, Chile: ECLAC.

ECLAC. (2012). *Statistical yearbook for Latin American and the Caribbean 2011*. Retrieved May 2012 from http://www.eclac.cl/publicaciones/xml/8/45608/LCG2513b_1.pdf

Ganimian, A. J., & Solano Rocha, A. (2011). *Measuring up? How Did Latin America and the Caribbean perform on the 2009 programme for international student assessment (PISA)?* Santiago, Chile: PREAL. Retrieved April 2012 from http://www.thedialogue.org/PublicationFiles/Preal_PISA_ENGLowres.pdf

García de Fanelli, A. (2011a). La educación superior en Argentina-Informe Nacional. In J. J. Brunner & R. Ferrada Hurtado (Eds.), *Educación superior en Iberoamérica: Informe 2011*. Santiago, Chile: CINDA-UNIVERSIA.

García de Fanelli, A. (2011b). *Modelos institucionales, tendencias y desafíos de la educación superior técnica y tecnológica no universitaria en Brasil, Colombia y México* (Report). Buenos Aires, Argentina: IIPE-UNESCO-Paris.

García de Fanelli, A., & Jacinto, C. (2011). *La educación superior no universitaria en América Latina: equidad e inserción en el mercado de trabajo en países seleccionados* (Report). Buenos Aires, Argentina: IIPE-UNESCO Paris.

Gasparini, L., Galiani, S., Cruces, G., & Acosta, P. (2011). *Educational upgrading and returns to skills in Latin America: Evidence from a supply-demand framework, 1990-2010* (Policy Research Working Paper, No. 5921). Washington, DC: World Bank.

Graduados Colombia Observatorio Laboral. (2011a). *Porcentaje de graduados 2001–2009 que se encuentran vinculados al sector formal de la economía* (Report). Retrieved April 2011 from http://www.graduadoscolombia.edu.co/html/1732/article-195066.html

Graduados Colombia Observatorio Laboral. (2011b). *Salario de Entrada de los recién graduados de la educación superior* (Report). Retrieved April 2011 from http://www.graduadoscolombia.edu.co/html/1732/article-195406.html

Leal Lobo, R. (2011). La educación superior en Brasil-Informe Nacional. In J. J Brunner & R. Ferrada Hurtado (Eds.), *Educación superior en Iberoamérica: Informe 2011*. Santiago, Chile: CINDA-UNIVERSIA.

Meller, P., & Brunner, J. J. (Eds.). (2009). *Educación técnico profesional y mercado laboral en Chile: Un reader*. Santiago, Chile: MINEDUC- Ingeniería Industrial Universidad. Retrieved March 2012 from http://refugioenchile.cl/data/archivos/archivo_2011_08_22_16_54_27.pdf

Meller, P., Lara, B., & Valdés, G. (2009, October). *Comparación intertemporal de ingresos y probabilidad de empleo por carrera, al primer año de titulación*. Santiago, Chile: MINEDUC- Ingeniería Industrial Universidad. Retrieved March 2012 from http://www.mifuturo.cl/images/Estudios/Estudios_asociados_a_Futuro_Laboral/fl003.pdf

MINEDUC (2012). *Mi futuro laboral*. Santiago, Chile: MINEDUC. Retrieved June 2012 from http://www.mifuturo.cl/

ME (Ministerio de Educación de la Argentina). (2012). *Ingeniería*. Mimeo. Buenos Aires, Argentina: Ministerio de Educación.

Orozco Silva, L. E., Castillo Gómez, L. C., & Varelo, A. R. Educación Superior en Colombia-Informe Nacional. In J. J. Brunner, & R. Ferrada Hurtado (Eds.), *Educación superior en Iberoamérica: Informe 2011*. Santiago, Chile: CINDA-UNIVERSIA.

Scheele, J., & Brunner, J. J. (2009). *Educación terciaria y mercado laboral: Formación profesional, empleo y empleabilidad. Una revisión de la literatura internacional*. Santiago, Chile: MINEDUC-Universidad Diego Portales.

SEDLAC (Socio-Economic Database for Latin America and the Caribbean). (2011). *Wages per hour LAC*. Retrieved March 2011 from http://cedlas.econo.unlp.edu.ar/eng/index.php

Sinnott, E., Nash, J., & de la Torre, A. (2010). *Natural resources in Latin America: Beyond booms and busts?* Washington DC: World Bank.

Teichler, U. (2009). *Higher education and the world of work*. Rotterdam, The Netherlands: Sense.

Turbay, C. (2010). *Educación técnica y tecnológica superior en Colombia y sus efectos para la inserción laboral e inclusión social de las juventudes: Estudio de caso en tres instituciones de Bogotá-Distrito Capital* (Report). Bogota, Colombia: UNESCO-IIPE and Fundación Restrepo Barco.

UIS (UNESCO Institute of Statistics). (2012a). *Graduates by broad field of education in tertiary education*. Retrieved April 2012 from http://stats.uis.unesco.org/unesco/ReportFolders/ReportFolders.aspx

UIS (UNESCO Institute of Statistics). (2012b). *UNESCO eAtlas of research and experimental development*. Retrieved June 2012 from http://www.app.collinsindicate.com/uis-atlas-RD/en-us

U.S. Department of Labor. (2012). *Employment projections: Fastest growing occupations*. Retrieved June 2012 from http://www.bls.gov/emp/ep_table_103.htm

Zapata, G., Tejeda, I., & Álvaro, R. (2011). Educación superior en Chile-Informe Nacional. In J. J. Brunner & R. Ferrada Hurtado (Eds.), *Educación superior en Iberoamérica: Informe 2011*. Santiago, Chile: CINDA-UNIVERSIA.

Chapter Three

BUILDING KNOWLEDGE-BASED ECONOMIES IN LATIN AMERICA: THE ROLE OF NATIONAL STUDY ABROAD SCHOLARSHIP PROGRAMS

RAISA BELYAVINA AND JORDAN BRENSINGER, IIE

As societies and economies become more interdependent, more students are crossing national borders in pursuit of higher education. Like other world regions, Latin America has seen a rise in both interregional and intraregional student mobility. Countries in the region have long been committed to building knowledge-based economies and, in recent years, have allocated funds for their students to pursue international education opportunities abroad. The goal of these initiatives is to turn students into trained experts who will contribute to the further development of their home countries. This article provides a comprehensive overview of the major national-level scholarship schemes in Latin America that currently exist or are under consideration.

From 2005 to 2010, the number of students studying abroad increased 6 percent from just over 2,455,000 (UNESCO Institute for Statistics [UIS], 2006) to 4,100,000. (Organisation for Economic Co-operation and Development [OECD], 2012.) In large part, this trend reflects the changing landscape of financial resources available to students. In particular, an increased number of government-funded scholarship initiatives support study abroad in order to capitalize on the resulting growth in national human resources that impact domestic economic development. Examples include the China Scholarship Council's State-Sponsored Study Abroad

Programs, which between 1996 and 2005 sponsored more than 22,000 students for study abroad (China Scholarship Council, 2006); the scholarship programs of Iraq's Higher Committee for Education Development, the Ministry of Higher Education and Scientific Research, and the Kurdistan Regional Government's Human Capacity Development Program, which each committed to awarding about 1,000 scholarships in 2011 (Embassy of the United States Baghdad, Iraq, n.d.-1–3); and Saudi Arabia's monumental King Abdullah Scholarship Program, currently investing nearly $2.4 billion each year to send 125,000 Saudi students abroad ("Enormous Saudi Scholarship," 2012).

Interest in international education among students from Latin America has witnessed similar growth. Keeping pace with growth in other world regions, the number of Latin American students studying abroad increased from nearly 146,000 in 2004 to nearly 196,000 in 2009 (UIS, 2006, 2011), an increase of 34.5 percent. Despite this increase, Latin American students represented only 5.8 percent of total internationally mobile students in 2009, nearly the same rate as in 2004 (5.9 percent). As the following sections will show, Latin American governments recognize the importance to national development of providing their students high-quality educational and research opportunities. With domestic institutions sometimes lacking the capacity or quality of international universities, governments set about financing a new wave of their students. This chapter outlines the current landscape of national study-abroad scholarship programs in light of the global push for social and economic growth.

COUNTRY PROFILES

Brazil

In August 2011, when President Dilma Rousseff announced the launch of a $1.65 billion scholarship program ("Studying the World," 2012), the Brazilian government firmly established itself as a leading player in the use of study-abroad scholarships to stimulate national development. The Brazil Scientific Mobility Program seeks to "promote the consolidation and expansion of science, technology and innovation in Brazil by means of international exchange and mobility" (Science Without Borders, n.d.-2) in the hopes of transforming the country's system of research and development. (Science Without Borders, n.d.-4). In terms of its funding structure, the program embodies public–private partnership, with the Coordination for the Improvement of Higher Education Personnel (CAPES), a subsidiary of the Ministry of Education, and the National Counsel for Scientific and Technological Development (CNPq) within the Ministry of Science and Technology. The government and private sector plan to send a total of 101,000 individuals to top universities abroad by 2015

(Science Without Borders, n.d.-1), with three-quarters receiving government scholarships (Ciência sem Fronteiras, n.d.-2). To date, the Brazil Scientific Mobility Program has sent nearly 2,000 individuals to study in the United States alone (E. Monks, personal communication, August 9, 2012).

Unlike many of its counterparts around the world, the Brazil Scientific Mobility Program limits awardees to a maximum of one year of study in nondegree programs outside of Brazil, including the option for a summer internship, ranging from undergraduate studies to opportunities for visiting researchers and scholars. This reflects the government's belief in the importance of attaining degrees from Brazil's domestic universities. Awardees, selected from lists of top qualified students tendered by the universities, receive full tuition and other benefits.

Key to the mission of these scholarships is stimulating national growth and research and development. Applicants must select from a defined set of national priorities emphasizing science, technology, engineering, and mathematics (STEM) fields, ranging from computer science to energy innovation and marine science (Science Without Borders, n.d.-1). To minimize the loss of this expertise to other countries, the Brazilian government requires that scholarship recipients return to Brazil within three months of the completion of their studies and remain there for a minimum of two years (E. Monks, personal communication, August 9, 2012).

Having identified a scarcity of PhDs in the total population, the Brazilian government is increasing the number of highly trained Brazilian researchers and entrepreneurs and stemming Brazilian brain drain through its investment in scholarships for international study (Science Without Borders, n.d.-1, n.d.-2). As Brazil continues to become a key player within the international community, training students abroad works to "induce the internationalization of universities and research centers in Brazil by encouraging the establishment of international partnerships" (Science Without Borders, n.d.-3) and "promot[ing] international collaborations in scientific publications…[and] foster[ing] the rate of patent applications nationally and internationally" (Science Without Borders, n.d.-1).

Chile

In the past, a variety of Chilean government entities funded students to study abroad, including the former Ministry of Planning and Cooperation, the Higher Education Quality and Equity Improvement Program, the National Scientific and Technological Research Commission (*Comisión Nacional de Investigación Científica y Tecnológica*, or CONICYT), the Agency for International Cooperation, and the National Counsel of Culture and the Arts. Yet these funds only provided opportunities for approximately

200 individuals per year through 2007 (OECD & The World Bank, 2010). As in the case of Brazil, Chile sought to catalyze additional human resource capacity to promote the country's development. Launched in October 2008 by then President Michelle Bachelet by Supreme Decree number 664, the *Becas Chile* (Chile Scholarships) program aimed to fund 30,000 students for international study by 2017 (Downie, 2011). Through 2011, the program has offered 5,809 individuals the opportunity to study internationally (Ministerio de Educación [Ministry of Education], n.d.-3).

Of the programs outlined in this chapter, *Becas Chile* represents the largest government investment with a fund of $6 billion from the Chilean Ministry of Education (MINEDUC). With the interest from this fund, MINEDUC intends to eventually provide $250 million each year in support of 3,300 awardees (OECD & The World Bank, 2010, pp. 42–43), a significant increase over the aforementioned scholarships offered before the *Becas* program. Joint responsibility for funding and managing these new resources lies with the higher education division of CONICYT, the Center for Improvement, Experimentation and Research, and the Open Doors English Program, all subsidiaries of MINEDUC.

Becas Chile includes funding for 11 different subprograms, including study for traditional master's and doctoral programs and postdoctoral research, as well as for doctoral, technical, and mathematics and science internships ranging in length from three months for an internship in mathematics and the sciences (Ministerio de Educación, n.d.-5) to four years for a full doctoral program (Ministerio de Educación, n.d.-2). Some may include an additional period for language training (OECD & The World Bank, 2010, p. 45). The majority of these scholarships serve graduate students and professionals, with only the Semester Abroad for Students of English Teaching component offering funding for undergraduate study (Ministerio de Educación, n.d.-1).

Much like its counterparts elsewhere in Latin America, *Becas Chile* focuses on the economic, social, and cultural development of Chile by strengthening "basic and applied research, scientific and technological development, innovation and entrepreneurship" (Ministerio de Educación, n.d.-4). Unlike its Latin American neighbors, however, Chile does not attempt to achieve this primarily through funding specific fields that are of national priority. While some scholarships within the program correspond to subject areas—for example, teaching English or pursuing a Master of Education degree—the vast majority of scholarships are offered for master's and doctoral work (Ministerio de Educación, n.d.-3), allowing for complete flexibility for students regarding field of study (CONICYT, n.d.-9, n.d.-10). Rather, the program emphasizes the value of high-quality research, teaching, and technical abilities, regardless of subject area. In endeavoring to ensure the high quality of its international opportunities and to promote the development of talented students and researchers, *Becas Chile* also requires that applicants' target institutions rank within the top 150 of the Times Higher Education World University Rankings or the Academic Ranking of World Universities, or place within the top 50 for the particular field of study chosen by the applicant (CONICYT, n.d.-1–8).

Ever important to the development of national human resource capacity, scholarship recipients may remain abroad after completion of their program for up to half the period of funding, at which time they must return to the country and spend a minimum of two years there for each year of scholarship funding, one if the work takes place outside the capital. Other obligations apply, depending on the award and level of education. Despite these measures, during its review of *Becas Chile* in 2009, the OECD recommended the implementation of additional incentives in order to effectively encourage awardees to return home (OECD & The World Bank, 2010, p. 18).

Colombia

The National Program for the Formation of Researchers, also known as *Becas Colciencias* (Colciencias Scholarships), a program of the Administrative Department of Science, Technology and Innovation (*Departamento Administrativo de Ciencia, Tecnología e Innovación,* or Colciencias for short), serves as the Colombian government's effort to advance higher education opportunities for Colombian students, both domestically and internationally, with the goal of expediting the country's development. Underlying this Colombian initiative is the desire to "foster excellent researchers in order to increase the national research and innovation capacities of . . . businesses, research centers and universities, among others" (Colciencias, n.d.-2). The Colombian government hopes to train 3,600 more doctoral students in the years leading up to 2019 (Colciencias, n.d.-1). In 2012, the program sponsored 800 students for doctoral studies, nearly 500 of whom studied abroad (Colciencias, 2012b). For 2013, *Becas Colciencias* will offer 475 million pesos, or nearly $36.2 million, in scholarship assistance for Colombian doctoral students to go abroad (Colciencias, 2012a).

The Administrative Department of Science, Technology and Innovation (Colciencias), from which the program receives its name, funds and manages the scholarships, in some cases collaborating with the Foundation for the Future of Colombia. At the same time, Colciencias maintains partnerships specifically with the French government and Fulbright Colombia and Purdue University in the United States. As a result, students studying in France are eligible for predoctorate French training and visa assistance, while their counterparts going to study in the United States receive a host of benefits including funds, language training, and visa assistance (Colciencias, 2012a). Through its relationship with Purdue University, Colciencias supports the areas of nanotechnology, biotechnology, biodiversity, environmental sustainability, and engineering to counter natural disasters and engineering and science education (Colciencias, n.d.-3).

Becas Colciencias seeks to strengthen Colombia's human capital resources to transform the country into a center for research and innovation and improve its competitiveness, while improving social equity and quality of life for all Colombians (Colciencias, n.d.-1). As the emphasis on doctoral students above might suggest, the Colombian government "considers the formation of doctors [PhDs] one of the most important strategies for strengthening the [country's] research capacities" (Colciencias, n.d.-1, p. 1). Of similar importance to the character of the program, studies must align with certain national priority areas focusing on science, technology, and national development, including electrical and renewable energy, aerospace, automotive engineering, the pharmaceutical industry, agroindustry, infrastructure, regional or national social and economic development, public policy, and restructuring of the state (Colciencias, n.d.-1).

Unlike many of its counterparts in Latin America, *Becas Colciencias* functions as a forgivable loan rather than an upfront grant. Awardees are given the opportunity to fulfill certain specific conditions, upon which the government will discharge all, or part, of their loan commitment. Forgiveness of 80 percent of an individual's loan depends on completing the degree, obtaining the corresponding credential, returning to Colombia within 30 days of program completion, and remaining in Colombia for at least two years and working in fields related to science, technology, or innovation (Colciencias, 2012a). The remaining 20 percent may be discharged depending on the nature of work completed in science, technology, or innovation. Awardees must complete two activities pertaining to an approved list of national priorities, including, among other things, strengthening the country's system of higher education at the graduate level, developing new products, and strengthening the research capacities of the country through publication. The awardee may forgo the completion of two activities through involvement in one new innovation or technology venture (Colciencias, 2012a).

Ecuador

Ecuador's National Secretariat for Higher Education, Science Technology and Innovation (*Secretaria Nacional de Educación Superior, Ciencia, Tecnología e Innovación*, or SENESCYT) currently operates three noteworthy scholarship programs dedicated to national development through offering Ecuadorian students the opportunity to study abroad. These programs established the goal of

> achieving another model of development, especially designed to face the difficulties of a world that passes through major crisis and that has few

possibilities for creating favorable conditions for life, especially for less educated, able and therefore more sensitive and vulnerable populations (SENESCYT, n.d.-1, p. 1).

By 2011, the Ecuadorian government had funded 499 scholarships for study abroad in the previous 15 years. That August, the country announced its most ambitious scholarship program yet, with the allocation of 1,070 awards for study abroad the same year (SENESCYT, n.d.-4). SENESCYT funded and operated Open Call 2012, as the program's current iteration is known, focusing on stimulating growth in graduate education and medical training abroad within the highest caliber of international institutions. These awards fund between one and five years for a master's degree, doctorate, postdoctorate, or medical specialization. The fields of study eligible for these awards of full tuition and benefits fall into five categories, including life sciences, natural resource sciences, production and innovation sciences, social sciences, and art and culture. Scholarship hopefuls must apply to a list of top universities preapproved for Open Call 2012 and appended to the scholarship application (SENESCYT, n.d.-1).

To prevent brain drain, Ecuador also requires Open Call 2012 applicants to fulfill certain conditions before and after receiving the award. Unique to this program, individuals must provide a guarantor with assets valued at or above the total value of the scholarship unless proven incapable of doing so. In the event that a recipient fails to uphold the scholarship contract, his or her guarantor would be forced to assume responsibility for any remaining obligations. Recipients must also agree to return to Ecuador upon completion of their studies for a period of at least twice the duration of the award (SENESCYT, n.d.-1, p. 12).

The second program funded by SENESCYT, Universities of Excellence (*Universidades de Excelencia*), strives to make attendance at the world's top 175 universities possible for all interested and capable Ecuadorian graduate and undergraduate students (SENESCYT, n.d.-5). The scholarship offers full funding and benefits up to a maximum $250,000 for studies and research from the undergraduate to postdoctorate levels, including medical specializations. Periods of study vary in length from a minimum of one year for a medical specialization to a maximum of seven years for an undergraduate degree. As with Open Call 2012, applicants to Universities of Excellence must focus on a field within one of the five categories of national priority, provide a guarantor, and return to Ecuador for a minimum of twice the duration of government scholarship funding (SENESCYT, n.d.-3).

Recognizing that a shortage of strong English-teaching methodology hinders the learning of English language in Ecuador, Teach English (*Enseña Inglés*), the last of the three major Ecuadorian scholarship programs, offers upper-level secondary school students and undergraduate students funds for overseas study, in order to prepare the next generation of English teachers. Awards amount to approximately $33,000 for up to nine months of English language study in a recognized international institution (SENESCYT, n.d.-2).

As with the other Ecuadorian programs, awardees in the Teach English program must also have a guarantor. In addition, awardees must achieve at least a grade of B during their studies and return to Ecuador after completing the program to serve as English teachers for a minimum of two years at the upper-secondary or undergraduate level (SENESCYT, n.d.-2).

Other Programs

In addition to the major initiatives outlined above, a number of other Latin American governments use scholarship programs for study abroad as a means to encourage national development. In 2001, the Salvadorian government devoted funds from the privatization of the National Telecommunications Administration to the establishment of *Becas Fantel*, a program designed to support talented Salvadorians to study at domestic or international universities (FEDISAL, n.d.-2). Managed by the Foundation for Salvadorian Comprehensive Education (*Fundación para la Educación Integral Salvadoreña*, or FEDISAL), a private, nonprofit organization, *Becas Fantel* has sponsored over 900 students since 2002, with nearly 250 studying abroad (FEDISAL, n.d.-1). While the program has offered 35 scholarships a year for study abroad, plans include expanding this number to 150 over the next three years (Downie, 2011).

Launched more than 40 years ago, the program, Mexico's Scholarship Program for Graduate Studies (*Programa de Becas para Estudios de Posgrado*), funded and administered by the National Council for Science and Technology (*Consejo Nacional de Ciencia y Tecnología*, or CONACYT), strives to "contribute to the formation of high-level scientists and technologists and increase the scientific and technological capacity of Mexico" through both domestic and international studies (CONACYT, 2012b). It offers up to two years for master's study, five years for doctoral study, and one year for university specialties, which include undergraduate studies (CONACYT, 2012a).

Other countries are considering the expansion of current programs or establishment of new ones. The Peruvian government, for instance, may expand the country's national scholarship program, PRONABEC—a program devoted to supporting talented underprivileged students in STEM fields for study within the country and referred to as *Beca 18*—to include study abroad (H. Harmon, personal communication, August 10, 2012).

Common Themes

Across Latin America, governments are introducing national scholarship programs for study abroad as a means to stimulate domestic social and economic development. A number of common themes emerge from a close look at these programs:

- National economic development is a driving priority for investment in higher education.
- A strong emphasis is put on graduate education and research, in addition to providing opportunities for undergraduate students.
- Extensive resources include full or nearly full funding and benefits for students.
- Postcompletion return requirements are often for double the award duration.

National Economic Development, a Driving Priority

National economic, social, and cultural development occupies a central position in the rationales and structures of the scholarship programs described in this chapter. The Brazil Scientific Mobility Program fills the need for "a new program to strongly encourage the internationalization of technology and innovation" (Science Without Borders, n.d.-3). *Becas Chile*, like its Brazilian counterpart, seeks to "define a comprehensive long-term policy for advanced human-capital formation abroad that allows Chile to join the knowledge society, thereby giving [the country] a definite impulse for economic, social and cultural development" (CONICYT, n.d.-10, p. 3). One of the two main goals of El Salvador's *Becas Fantel* is to "promote high-quality professional formation and specialization among Salvadorans with the end of contributing to the development of the country" (FEDISAL, n.d.-2). A few of the programs also recognize the need for providing opportunities for socioeconomically disadvantaged groups as part of their overarching goal of national development. In facilitating Colombia's national scholarship program, *Colciencias* underscores the need for "human capital of a higher level that will contribute to the strengthening of the research and innovation capacities of the [Colombian] institutions. . . all with a view toward achieving 'a higher level of equity' and improving . . . the quality of life for all citizens" (Colciencias, n.d.-2, p. 1). Ecuador puts forth the goal of "achieving another model of development, especially designed to face the difficulties of a world that passes through major crisis and that has few possibilities for creating favorable conditions for life, especially for less educated, able and therefore more sensitive and vulnerable populations" (SENESCYT, n.d.-1, p. 1). Although each program reflects nuanced views regarding national development and how it should be pursued, their language and structures nevertheless revolve around this key priority of their funding governments.

Emphasis on Graduate Education and Research
While the scholarship programs described in this chapter include funds for studies ranging from upper-secondary school to postdoctoral research and technical education, these programs generally reserve a special role for graduate and postgraduate work. Three of the six programs in the profiled countries include some level of funding for the undergraduate level, and five include awards for graduate work. These investments indicate a view that undergraduate education and graduate education in particular are seen as the pillars of national social and economic development.

Extensive Resources for Funding and Benefits
Strong financial support for each of the highlighted programs has allowed students to obtain full or nearly full funding for some of the best higher education institutions around the world. These programs recognize that student expenses include far more than tuition and educational fees: Most programs include roundtrip airfare, a living allowance, and health care, among other benefits. A significant body of research suggests that financial concerns greatly impact students' ability to study abroad (e.g., see Belyavina & Bhandari, 2011; Carter, 1991; Kasravi, 2009; Salisbury, Umbach, Paulsen, & Pascarella, 2009; Van Der Meid, 2003). These scholarship schemes likely mitigate the financial challenges by offering full funding.

Postcompletion Return Requirements
Ensuring that the newly developed expertise is brought back into the domestic economy constitutes an important step in developing the human resources capacity for national growth (OECD & The World Bank, 2010). Each of the profiled scholarship programs recognizes the importance of the return of its award recipients and includes measures, whether rewarding or punitive, to draw awardees back to their country of origin. Nearly all of the programs require that scholarship recipients remain in the country for double the duration of their awards.

At the same time, a number of factors differentiate the programs from one another and offer insight into country-specific forms of structuring scholarship funds. While international scholarship programs are often focused on promoting mobility of students in the STEM fields, a number of scholarship schemes in Latin America encompass a broader range of fields of study, including social sciences, art and culture in the Ecuador programs, and complete flexibility of study with most *Becas Chile* scholarships.

Eligible universities in which Latin American students can pursue their course of study under government scholarships may or may not be restricted to the world's top-ranked institutions, depending on the country. Chile and Ecuador, for example, require that students apply to top institutions as outlined in a proprietary list and two major university ranking systems.

The length of study also varies from program to program. Nearly all the programs described in this chapter include funds for the obtaining of degrees abroad. The largest of those programs, the Brazil Scientific Mobility Program, is the exception. To stimulate the degree output of domestic institutions, Brazil remains committed to drawing scholarship recipients back to the country after one year of study abroad so that students receive their degrees from Brazilian higher education institutions.

The return of award recipients to their country of origin is of great importance to the success of national scholarship programs. While most of the programs described in this chapter employ upfront grants with penalties for a breach of contract, Colombia's *Becas Colciencias* functions as a forgivable loan, using incentives to encourage program completion and return to the country. Although the relative effectiveness of these strategies remains unclear, in at least one instance, the OECD recommended the use of positive, rather than negative, coercion in order to avoid the brain drain of scholars and researchers (OECD & The World Bank, 2010, p. 117). Should the Colombian strategies prove to work well, Colombia may become a model for other Latin American governments to emulate.

Similarly, the content of postaward requirements differs among the programs. Chile incentivizes working in underprivileged areas of the country by halving the work requirement for individuals working outside of the capital. In Colombia awardees under *Becas Colciencias* must not only return to the country for a given period of time, but also achieve certain field-specific goals in order to discharge the full loan amount.

Conclusions

The current emphasis on international study as a means to advance national economic growth attracts considerable attention from many Latin American governments. Billions of dollars enable students in a range of programs and fields of study to pursue high-quality training at universities around the world. The trajectory of such initiatives clearly points upward as existing programs announce expansions and more governments contemplate starting their own programs.

Furthermore, the similarities and differences in leading programs across the region offer insight into how governments are currently utilizing scholarships for national development. Initiatives devoted to graduate education, combined with certain restrictions or incentives, seek to catalyze the research and human resource capacities of burgeoning economies. Countries, however, continue to grapple with the complexity of student mobility and the various forces that seek to capitalize on it. The success or failure of governments to identify national priorities and encourage award recipients to participate in fostering them may determine whether Latin America's development follows the same upward path as their scholarships.

REFERENCES

Belyavina, R., & Bhandari, R. (2011). Increasing diversity in international careers: Economic challenges and solutions. *Partners Soar, 9*, 2–8. Retrieved from http://www.iie.org/Research-and-Publications/Publications-and-Reports/IIE-Bookstore/Increasing-Diversity-International-Education

Carter, H. (1991). Minority access to international education. In Council on International Educational Exchange, *Black students and overseas programs: Broadening the base of participation* (pp. 6–13). Retrieved from http://www.ciee.org/research_center/archive/CIEE_Education_Abroad_Informational_Documents/1991BlackStudentsOverseas.pdf

China Scholarship Council. (2006, July 20). *CSC 10th anniversary celebration held in Beijing.* Retrieved from http://en.csc.edu.cn/News/e659b51140a14890aca4631e83a7f56f.shtml

Ciência sem Fronteiras [Science Without Borders]. (n.d.-1). *Instituições de destino* [Destination institutions]. Retrieved from http://www.cienciasemfronteiras.gov.br/web/csf/instituicoes-de-destino1

Ciência sem Fronteiras [Science Without Borders]. (n.d.-2). *Metas* [Goals]. Retrieved from http://www.cienciasemfronteiras.gov.br/web/csf/metas

Comisión Nacional de Investigación Científica y Tecnológica [National Scientific and Technological Research Commission] [CONICYT]. (n.d.-1). *Bases concurso becas de doctorado en el extranjero Becas Chile Convocatoria 2012* [Guidelines for scholarship competition for doctorate abroad Chile Scholarships Call 2012]. Retrieved from http://www.conicyt.cl/573/articles-39819_bases.pdf

Comisión Nacional de Investigación Científica y Tecnológica [National Scientific and Technological Research Commission] [CONICYT]. (n.d.-2). *Bases concurso becas de magíster en el extranjero Becas Chile Convocatoria 2012* [Guidelines for competitive scholarships for master's abroad Chile Scholarships Call 2012]. Retrieved from http://www.mineduc.cl/usuarios/bchile/doc/201203211401150.BASES_MAG_2012_FINAL.pdf

Comisión Nacional de Investigación Científica y Tecnológica [National Scientific and Technological Research Commission] [CONICYT]. (n.d.-3). *Bases concurso becas de magíster en el extranjero para profesionales de la educación Becas Chile Convocatoria 2012* [Guidelines for competitive scholarships for master's abroad for education professionals Chile Scholarships Call 2012]. Retrieved from http://www.mineduc.cl/usuarios/bchile/doc/201208141628400.BASES_MG_PROF_EDUC_CONVOCATORIA_2012.pdf

Comisión Nacional de Investigación Científica y Tecnológica [National Scientific and Technological Research Commission] [CONICYT]. (n.d.-4). *Bases concurso becas para pasantías de perfeccionamiento de competencias técnicas en el extranjero: Becas Chile Convocatoria 2012* [Guidelines for competitive scholarships for technological competency improvement internships abroad: Chile Scholarships Call 2012]. Retrieved from http://www.mineduc.cl/usuarios/bchile/doc/201207231053550.BASES_PASANT_TECNICAS_FINAL.pdf

Comisión Nacional de Investigación Científica y Tecnológica [National Scientific and Technological Research Commission] [CONICYT]. (n.d.-5). *Beca de cotutela de doctorado en el extranjero Becas Chile bases concursales Convocatoria 2012* [Scholarship for doctoral co-supervision abroad Chile Scholarships competitive guidelines Call 2012]. Retrieved from http://www.conicyt.cl/573/articles-40662_bases.pdf

Comisión Nacional de Investigación Científica y Tecnológica [National Scientific and Technological Research Commission] [CONICYT]. (n.d.-6). *Beca de pasantía doctoral en el extranjero Becas Chile bases concursales Convocatoria 2012* [Scholarship for doctoral internship abroad Chile Scholarships competitive guidelines Call 2012]. Retrieved from http://www.mineduc.cl/usuarios/bchile/doc/ 201205172015230.BASES_PASANT_DOC_2012.pdf

Comisión Nacional de Investigación Científica y Tecnológica [National Scientific and Technological Research Commission] [CONICYT]. (n.d.-7). *Beca de postdoctorado en el extranjero Becas Chile: Bases concursales: Convocatoria 2012* [Scholarship for postdoctorate abroad Chile Scholarships: Competitive guidelines: Call 2012]. Retrieved from http://www.mineduc.cl/usuarios/bchile/doc/ 201205302010380.BASES_FINAL_POSTDOCTORADO_2012.pdf

Comisión Nacional de Investigación Científica y Tecnológica [National Scientific and Technological Research Commission] [CONICYT]. (n.d.-8). *Beca de subspecialidades médicas en el extranjero Becas Chile: Bases concursales: Convocatoria 2012* [Scholarship for medical subspecializations abroad Chile Scholarships: Competitive guidelines: Call 2012]. Retrieved from http://www.mineduc.cl/usuarios/bchile/doc/ 201206141340130.BASES_FINAL_SUBESP_MEDICA_2012.pdf

Comisión Nacional de Investigación Científica y Tecnológica [National Scientific and Technological Research Commission] [CONICYT]. (n.d.-9). *Becas de doctorado en el extranjero Becas Chile Convocatoria 2012* [Master's scholarships for study abroad Chile Scholarships Call 2012]. Retrieved from http://www.conicyt.cl/573/article-39819.html

Comisión Nacional de Investigación Científica y Tecnológica [National Scientific and Technological Research Commission] [CONICYT]. (n.d.-10). *Becas de magíster en el extranjero Becas Chile Convocatoria 2012* [Master's scholarships for study abroad Chile Scholarships Call 2012]. Retrieved from http://www.conicyt.cl/573/article-40474.html

Consejo Nacional de Ciencia y Tecnología [National Council for Science and Technology] [CONACYT]. (2012a, July 12). *Aspirantes a beca posgrados en el extranjero* [Applicants for graduate study-abroad scholarships]. Retrieved from http://www.conacyt.gob.mx/Becas/Aspirantes/Paginas/Becas_AspirantesExtranjero.aspx

Consejo Nacional de Ciencia y Tecnología [National Council for Science and Technology] [CONACYT]. (2012b, July 12). *Becas para estudios de posgrado* [Scholarships for graduate studies]. Retrieved from http://www.conacyt.gob.mx/Becas/Paginas/Default.aspx

Departamento Administrativo de Ciencia, Tecnología e Innovación [Administrative Department of Science, Technology and Innovation] [Colciencias]. (n.d.-1). *Convocatoria nacional para estudios de doctorado en el extranjero año 2012: conformación de un banco de elegibles* [National call for doctoral studies abroad 2012: confirmation of eligible bank]. Retrieved from http://www.colciencias.gov.co/sites/default/files/upload/ documents/tdr_doctorados_exterior.pdf

Departamento Administrativo de Ciencia, Tecnología e Innovación [Administrative Department of Science, Technology and Innovation] [Colciencias]. (n.d.-2). *Formación de investigadores* [Formation of researchers]. Retrieved from http://www.colciencias.gov.co/programa_estrategia/formaci-n-de-investigadores

Departamento Administrativo de Ciencia, Tecnología e Innovación [Administrative Department of Science, Technology and Innovation] [Colciencias]. (n.d.-3). *Anexo programa de cooperación Purdue University* [Annex for the Purdue University cooperation program]. Retrieved from http://www.colciencias.gov.co/sites/default/ files/upload/complementary/anexo_de_cooperacion_purdue_university.pdf

Departamento Administrativo de Ciencia, Tecnología e Innovación [Administrative Department of Science, Technology and Innovation] [Colciencias]. (2012a). *Anexo No. 1: Reglamento de operación del crédito educativo condonable para la realización de estudios de doctorado en el exterior – año 2012* [Annex No. 1: Rules of operation for the forgivable educational credit for the realization of doctoral studies abroad – 2012]. Retrieved from http://www.colciencias.gov.co/sites/default/files/upload/complementary/anexo_1_instructivo_exterior_ano_2012.pdf

Departamento Administrativo de Ciencia, Tecnología e Innovación [Administrative Department of Science, Technology and Innovation] [Colciencias]. (2012b, April 2). *Este año Colciencias entregará 800 becas para estudios doctorales* [This year Colciencias will give 800 scholarships for doctoral studies]. Retrieved from http://www.colciencias.gov.co/noticias/este-o-colciencias-entregar-800-becas-para-estudios-doctorales

Downie, A. (2011, August 9). Latin American countries push more students to study abroad. *The Chronicle of Higher Education.* Retrieved from http://chronicle.com/article/Latin-American-Countries-Push/128584/

Embassy of the United States Baghdad, Iraq. (n.d.-1). *Government of Iraq Ministry of Higher Education and Scientific Research programs.* Baghdad, Iraq: Embassy of the United States.

Embassy of the United States Baghdad, Iraq. (n.d.-2). *Higher Committee for Education Development in Iraq.* Baghdad, Iraq: Embassy of the United States.

Embassy of the United States Baghdad, Iraq. (n.d.-3). *Human capacity development program: Kurdistan Regional Government (KRG), Iraq.* Baghdad, Iraq: Embassy of the United States.

Enormous Saudi scholarship programme extended to 2020. (2012, February 27). *ICEF Monitor.* Retrieved from http://monitor.icef.com/2012/02/enormous-saudi-scholarship-programme-in-the-spotlight/

Fundación para la Educación Integral Salvadoreña [Salvadoran Comprehensive Education Foundation] [FEDISAL]. (n.d.-1). *Estadísticas* [Statistics]. Retrieved from http://www.fedisal.org.sv/fantel/IH_ShowContenido.aspx?id=Estadisticas

Fundación para la Educación Integral Salvadoreña [Salvadoran Comprehensive Education Foundation] [FEDISAL]. (n.d.-2). *Objetivos* [Objectives]. Retrieved from http://www.fedisal.org.sv/fantel/IH_Inicio.aspx?page=paginas/ objetivos.html

Kasravi, J. (2009). *Factors influencing the decision to study abroad for students of color: Moving beyond the barriers.* (Doctoral dissertation, University of Minnesota). Retrieved from http://conservancy.umn.edu/bitstream/55058/1/Kasravi_umn_0130E_10602.pdf

Ministerio de Educación [Ministry of Education]. (n.d.-1). *Becas de pedagogía: Información general* [Teaching scholarships: General information]. Retrieved from http://www.becaschile.cl/index2.php?id_portal=60&id_seccion=3519&id_contenido=14641

Ministerio de Educación [Ministry of Education]. (n.d.-2). *Becas de postgrado: Información general* [Graduate scholarships: General information]. Retrieved from http://www.becaschile.cl/index2.php?id_portal=60&id_seccion=3517&id_contenido=14639

Ministerio de Educación [Ministry of Education]. (n.d.-3). *Estadísticas generales* [General statistics]. Retrieved from http://www.becaschile.cl/index2.php?id_portal=60&id_seccion=3536&id_contenido=15472

Ministerio de Educación [Ministry of Education]. (n.d.-4). *Objetivos* [Objectives]. Retrieved from http://www.becaschile.cl/index2.php?id_portal=60&id_seccion=3530&id_contenido=14555

Ministerio de Educación [Ministry of Education]. (n.d.-5). *Pasantías de matemáticas y ciencias* [Mathematics and science internships]. Retrieved from http://www.becaschile.cl/index2.php?id_seccion=3519&id_portal=60&id_contenido=14595

OECD & The World Bank. (2010). *Reviews of national policies for education: Chile's international scholarship programme.* Paris, France: OECD.

OECD. (2012). *Education at a glance 2012.* Paris, France: OECD.

Salisbury, M. H., Umbach, P. D., Paulsen, M. B., & Pascarella, E. T. (2009). Going global: Understanding the choice process of the intent to study abroad. *Research in Higher Education, 50,* 119–143. doi: 10.1007/s11162-008-9111-x

Science Without Borders. (n.d.-1) FAQ. Retrieved from http://www.cienciasemfronteiras.gov.br/web/csf-eng/faq

Science Without Borders. (n.d.-2). Goals. Retrieved from http://www.cienciasemfronteiras.gov.br/web/csf-eng/goals

Science Without Borders. (n.d.-3) Motivation. Retrieved from http://www.cienciasemfronteiras.gov.br/web/csf-eng/motivation

Science Without Borders. (n.d.-4). The program. Retrieved from http://www.cienciasemfronteiras.gov.br/web/csf-eng/home

Secretaria Nacional de Educación Superior, Ciencia, Tecnología e Innovación [National Secretary of Higher Education, Science, Technology and Innovation] [SENESCYT]. (n.d.-1). *Bases de postulación: Programa de Becas "Convocatoria Abierta 2012 Segunda Fase"* [Application guidelines: Scholarship Program "Open Call 2012 Second Phase"]. Retrieved from http://www.senescyt.gob.ec/c/document_library/get_file?uuid=9c438150-ab3e-43b8-b5f2-60105c1822eb&groupId=240658

Secretaria Nacional de Educación Superior, Ciencia, Tecnología e Innovación [National Secretary of Higher Education, Science, Technology and Innovation] [SENESCYT]. (n.d.-2). *Bases de postulación: Programa de Becas "Docentes de Inglés para 8° Año de Educación General Básica (EGB) a 3° de Bachillerato en Establecimientos Fiscales – Enseña Inglés"* [Application guidelines: Scholarship Program "Students of English for the 8th Year of General Basic Education (EGB) to the 3rd year of Baccalaureate in Fiscal Establishments – Teach English"]. Retrieved from http://www.senescyt.gob.ec/Convocatoria_Ingles/adjuntos/ Bases_de_Postulacion.pdf

Secretaria Nacional de Educación Superior, Ciencia, Tecnología e Innovación [National Secretary of Higher Education, Science, Technology and Innovation] [SENESCYT]. (n.d.-3). *Bases de postulación: Programa de Becas "Universidades de Excelencia"* [Application guidelines: Scholarship Program "Universities of Excellence"]. Retrieved from http://www.senescyt.gob.ec/c/document_library/get_file?uuid=48e90cc1-4acf-4db0-81ca-7e6d3196dc3a&groupId=240658

Secretaria Nacional de Educación Superior, Ciencia, Tecnología e Innovación [National Secretary of Higher Education, Science, Technology and Innovation] [SENESCYT]. (n.d.-4). *SENESCYT comple objetivo histórico para la educación superior del país* [SENESCYT achieves historic objective for the country's higher education]. Retrieved from http://www.senescyt.gob.ec/web/guest/305

Secretaria Nacional de Educación Superior, Ciencia, Tecnología e Innovación [National Secretary of Higher Education, Science, Technology and Innovation] [SENESCYT]. (n.d.-5). *Universidades de Excelencia* [Universities of Excellence]. Retrieved from http://www.senescyt.gob.ec/web/240658/23

Studying the world: A huge scholarship programme could boost economic growth. (2012, March 17). *The Economist.* Retrieved from http://www.economist.com/node/21550306

UNESCO Institute for Statistics (UIS). (2006). *Global education digest 2006: Comparing education statistics across the world.* Montreal, Canada: UIS. Retrieved from http://www.uis.unesco.org/Library/Documents/ged06-en.pdf

UNESCO Institute for Statistics (UIS). (2011). *Global education digest 2011: Comparing education statistics across the world.* Montreal, Canada: UIS.

Van Der Meid, J. S. (2003). Asian Americans: Factors influencing the decision to study abroad. *Frontiers 9*(4), 71–110. Retrieved from http://www.frontiersjournal.com/issues/vol9/vol9-04_vandermeid.pdf

Chapter Four

BREAKING DOWN SOCIETAL BARRIERS: INCREASING ACCESS AND EQUITY TO HIGHER EDUCATION IN LATIN AMERICA

OSCAR ESPINOZA, UNIVERSIDAD UCINF, CHILE

This chapter will describe and analyze how government policies address the challenge of equity in higher education and the directions that now characterize its evolution, especially with regard to student support schemes. The chapter will focus primarily on equity in access to higher education.[1]

This chapter is organized into three sections: The first provides the theoretical framework guiding the analysis. It discusses the concepts of equity and equality and their implications. The second section presents a model for analyzing equity and highlights the policies of equity and inclusion in higher education throughout Latin America. The third section discusses the results derived from implemented equity policies and strategies.

Understanding the Relevance and Origins of Equity and Equality

In this section, the meaning, goals, and assumptions of equity and equality will be considered in terms of their implications for social and educational policy. Instead of arguing for a simple conception of equity and equality, a set of definitions of those concepts, as well as a discussion related to associated theoretical and policy issues, will be presented. Moreover, a model for analyzing equity and equality in relation to education will be discussed.

Equity and equality must be considered as the basis for distributive justice, which Morton Deutsch (1975, 137) noted "is concerned with the distribution of the conditions and goods which affect individual well-being." Deutsch (137–138) argued that "the sense of injustice with regard to the distribution of benefits and harms, rewards and costs, or other things which affect individual well-being may be directed at: (a) the values underlying the rules governing the distribution (injustice of values), (b) the rules which are employed to represent the values (injustice of rules), (c) the ways that the rules are implemented (injustice of implementation), or (d) the way decisions are made about any of the foregoing (injustice of decision-making procedures)."

In debates about distributive justice, the word *equity* is often used as if it were interchangeable with *equality* (Lerner, 1974; Warner, 1985). However, Secada (1989) argued that equality is not synonymous with equity; thus, rather than striving for equality among groups of people, we should work toward equitable inequalities that reflect the needs and strengths of the various groups. Secada posited that students' needs must be addressed on an individual level. Unfortunately, human beings are creatures of bias, and thus certain inequalities are bound to exist. When a particular group is treated with inequality, it is important to examine the source of inequality and determine the reasons for it.

The concept of equity is associated with fairness and justice and takes individual circumstances into consideration, while equality usually connotes sameness in treatment by asserting the fundamental or natural equality of all persons (Corson, 2001).

The Equity Model

The equity goal-oriented model represents my understanding of educational equity goals. It attempts to facilitate the efforts of researchers and evaluators to critically examine and synthesize equity-based research.

TABLE 4.1: THE EQUITY MODEL: A MULTIDIMENSIONAL APPROACH

Dimensions	Resources	Features or Stages of the Educational Process			
		Access	Survival (educational attainment)	Performance	Outcomes
Equity for equal needs	Guarantee that all people who have same needs have same amount of resources (*The reasonable classification definition*; see Carlson, 1983).	Provide access at the individual and group level on the basis of need (i.e., the same level of access to quality education for those with same needs and different level of access for those with different needs (*The goal-oriented definition*; see Harvey & Klein, 1985).	Ensure that those with equal needs gain equal level of educational attainment.	Ensure that every individual is enabled to obtain a minimal achievement level (*The minimum achievement definition*; see Gordon, 1972) and that differences in achievement beyond that are based on need.	Ensure that those with equal needs obtain equal jobs, income, and political power.
Equity for equal potential (abilities)	Ensure that all individuals with certain potential have same amount resources (*The full opportunity definition*; see Tumin, 1965, cited in Carlson, 1983).	Guarantee that all individuals who have equal abilities will gain access to quality education.	Ensure that students with equal potential realize equal educational attainment.	Ensure that students with similar abilities will have similar academic performance.	Ensure that those with equal potential obtain equal jobs, income, and political power.
Equity for equal achievement	Ensure that individuals who achieve or whose parents achieve the same level would have equal resources.	Provide equal access to quality education for students having equal past achievements.	Ensure that students with similar qualifications will stay in the system (*The competition definition*; see Warner, Havighurst, & Loeb, 1944).	Ensure equal achievement for those who have achieved the same academic performance in the past.	Ensure that individuals with similar academic achievement will obtain similar job statuses, incomes, and political power.

Source: Espinoza (2002, 2007).

Table 4.1 portrays the model in a matrix format. The columns of the matrix are defined by the resources (financial, social, and cultural) and the main facets of the educational process: access, survival (educational attainment), performance (educational achievement based on test performance), and outcome (occupational status, income, and political power). The rows of the matrix distinguish three equity dimensions at the individual and group levels: (1) equity for equal needs, (2) equity for equal potential, and (3) equity for equal achievement.

Policies and Strategies of Equity and Inclusion in Higher Education

Several developing countries' governments, particularly in Latin America, as well as some international organizations such as the UNESCO International Institute for Higher Education in Latin America and the Caribbean (UNESCO/IESALC), Organisation for Economic Co-operation and Development (OECD), the Center for Interuniversity Development (CINDA), and the World Bank, have conceptualized aspects of equity and inclusion. Developing countries are facing a series of challenges with regard to equity and inclusion policies in higher education, such as:

- To deepen equity policies for entrance and instrument new mechanisms of public support for students (scholarships and student loans, health and nutrition services, cultural activities, student residences, academic support, etc.) aimed at enabling their permanence and good performance in the systems.

- To provide greater options for students within the system through flexible curricula that enable mobility and take into account their particular interests and vocations, and the access to new degree formations in line with the evolution of demands in the world of work.

- To advance toward better integrated tertiary education systems founded on diversity.

- To decentralize and regionalize educational offerings to ensure territorial equity and facilitate the incorporation of local actors.

- To articulate higher education policies with those addressed to the school system, contributing to the formation of solid cognitive and learning bases so that students entering the upper level have the values, skills, abilities, and capabilities to acquire, build, and transfer knowledge to benefit society.

- To provide timely and quality information about job opportunities.

- To ensure quality education for all from elementary to higher education. For this reason, access policies should also consider the need to implement quality programs of teaching and research at the postgraduate level.

Similarly, the OECD (2008) acknowledged several factors that affect the development and implementation of equity policies in the tertiary sector, namely, (a) factors associated with financing (e.g., availability of student aid programs), (b) family history, (c) school, (d) peers, (e) the link between secondary and tertiary education, (f) the organization of tertiary education, (g) selection procedures, and (h) factors impacting the participation of students with disabilities.

In this context, a set of policy guidelines was recently developed that aims to increase access for those most likely to be excluded. These guidelines specifically aim to do the following:

- Value the origin and scope of equity by generating a set of performance indicators that monitor access, participation, retention, and success of disadvantaged groups.

- Achieve greater equity in tertiary education by strengthening the efficiency and equity of school systems. This should include limiting early academic selection, providing necessary support to students at risk of dropping out, strengthening the links between the school and the families, and allocating resources to those most in need (OECD 2007a).

- Strengthen the orientation and vocational counseling services at the secondary level in order to ensure that the most economically and socially disadvantaged students have opportunities similar to their more advantaged peers to access tertiary education (OECD 2004b).

- Provide opportunities to study in tertiary education and at the vocational-technical level.

- Diversify higher education offerings in order to respond to the students' diverse backgrounds, experiences, skills, and aspirations.

- Meet the aspirations of different ethnic and cultural groups in society.

- Improve access to higher education in distant areas by creating distance learning centers, regional centers of learning, and self-maintenance grants to pay the living expenses of students studying in remote areas.

- Diversify the admission requirements and entrance procedures of higher education (beyond standardized income tests).

- Consider positive discrimination policies aimed at particular groups with clearly identified educational disadvantages.

- Consider different eligibility requirements. For example, institutions should consider using individual aptitude tests to certify the competence of individuals who have not completed secondary education.

- Provide incentives to institutions that promote access for disadvantaged groups.

- Continue efforts to improve gender parity at all levels of tertiary education and encourage men and women to pursue less traditional studies for their gender.

- Place greater emphasis on the equity of outcomes. This would entail greater tutorial support for students most at risk of failure.

In the same vein, the OECD (2008) identified a set of trends related to equity in higher education:

- In most countries there is little information on the level of inequity in tertiary education. Nevertheless, some countries recognize the importance of equity issues within tertiary education policies and gather systematic information about the main background characteristics of their tertiary students, including access, participation, retention, and graduation (Martin, 1994).

- There is significant evidence that shows that access to and participation in higher education is directly linked to the students' socioeconomic level (Espinoza, 2002; Espinoza, González, & Castillo, 2007; OECD, 2007b).

- The socioeconomic background of students who attend secondary education impacts their aspirations for access to tertiary education (OECD, 2004a).

- The most disadvantaged students are overrepresented among young people who are not eligible for access to tertiary education for failing to achieve the necessary qualifications.

- When gaining access to tertiary education, the most disadvantaged students mainly enroll in lower-prestige postsecondary educational institutions and in institutions oriented to technical and vocational training (Martins, Mauritti, & Costa, 2005).

- Women are still underrepresented in some areas, such as technology and engineering, and overrepresented in other areas, such as education and nursing.

- In some countries, the tertiary degrees obtained by women are undervalued by the labor market (Berner, 2002).

- The inclusion of ethnic minorities presupposes serious challenges for some countries, such as Chile and Mexico (Evans, 2004; Malatest, 2004).

In most countries there is little emphasis on equity associated with outcomes. Undoubtedly, equity policies implemented by most countries have been focused on access rather than outcomes. However, this trend is changing in some countries like Mexico, where mentoring programs have granted disadvantaged students access to mentors who support and guide them during the study period (OECD 2008).

Results of the Policies and Strategies of Equity and Inclusion in Higher Education in Latin America

To understand how educational policies promoted in recent decades by Latin American governments have had an impact on equity, three stages of the educational process will be taken into consideration: access, survival, and outcomes. Reliable and comparable information at the regional level is available only in relation to these stages.

Equity in Relation to Access and Survival

Study opportunities in postsecondary education systems in the region depend on the amount of academic offerings, which are mainly concentrated in the private sector, and the socioeconomic status of students. In this context, governments and institutions have been promoting and implementing different policies of inclusion and equity in access in order to meet the growing demands from the policy environment, which include affirmative action programs (Brazil, Chile, Mexico), scholarship programs and state credits, stronger credit programs related to banking, quota systems, and the like.

To implement these policies, diverse strategies have been established in Latin America. Three types of countries can be identified: (1) countries with no barriers for access (Argentina and Uruguay have unrestricted access schemes; however, they require selection tests in some careers); (2) countries with mixed systems (in the Dominican Republic there are no selective exams, but an orientation and measurement test are given to applicants who need special support); and (3) countries that have systems where access is channeled through selection tests (Chile, Brazil, Costa Rica, Mexico, and Venezuela). In contrast, private universities in Latin America use various admission criteria, and access is conditioned by the applicants' ability to pay and, in some of these institutions, by selection processes.

Another strategy to generate greater equity in access involves subsidies and special programs oriented toward the most vulnerable. For example, in Argentina the Educational Credit National Program is oriented toward vulnerable students in general, while the University Scholarships National Program has a subprogram oriented toward indigenous students. In Bolivia, public institutions grant food and travel subsidies to their students.

In Brazil, the Higher Education Financing Program helps with loans to economically disadvantaged students who are in fee-charging institutions. In turn, the University for All Program aims to make access to higher education possible for impoverished youth. It has study scholarships for students of African descent and indigenous people, which are given according to the proportion of these populations in their respective states.

Mexico has several programs that give economic support, preferably for career paths in which most of the graduates obtain jobs within six months. For example, Fonabec provides scholarships and loans to students attending the Technological Universities of the Ministry of Education. Another initiative is the Higher Studies Scholarship National Program, which encourages access to higher education for impoverished youths.

In Uruguay, to ensure equitable access to the system, the University of the Republic, the University Professionals Fund, and the Ministry of Education and Culture established the National Solidarity Fund, which is financed with contributions from graduates of the higher courses of the Professional-Technical Education Council and graduates of the University of the Republic. The resources are collected annually to finance scholarships for students with good academic performance and scarce economic resources.

Gender and Socioeconomic Level
The policies and strategies promoted by governments can be further separated into two key indicators: (a) undergraduate enrollment by gender and (b) coverage of higher education according to socioeconomic level.

In terms of access to the tertiary system by gender, Table 4.2 verifies that female participation has gradually been gaining ground in Latin America, standing at an average rate of about 50 percent of the total participation rate in this sector. Moreover, in countries like Brazil, Chile, and Paraguay in the period 2005–2009, the female participation rate grew more than the male.

TABLE 4.2: UNDERGRADUATE ENROLLMENT IN HIGHER EDUCATION IN LATIN AMERICA BY GENDER (2005–2009)

Countries	2005	% Women	2009	% Women
Argentina	2,082,577	58.7	...	...
Brazil	4,572,297	55.9	6,115,138	57.0
Chile	663,694	48.1	876,243	50.7
Colombia	1,223,594	51.3	1,570,447	50.5
Costa Rica	110,717	54.3	...	...
El Salvador	122,431	54.7	143,849	54.4
Mexico	2,384,858	50.3	2,705,190	50.2
Panama	126,242	61.2	135,209	59.6
Paraguay	156,167	52.3	236,194	58.2
Peru	909,315	50.0	...	...
Uruguay	...	...	161,459	62.7
Venezuela	...	...	2,123,041	...

Source: CINDA (2007, 2011).

Access to tertiary education in Latin America is conditioned by students' previous trajectory through primary and secondary education, which in turn is limited by the socioeconomic status and cultural capital of the families. While participation rates have significantly increased, shortening the participation gap between the least and highest incomes sectors, there is still a high percentage of young people who do not have access to tertiary education due to economic shortcomings.

In terms of socioeconomic level, there is a close relationship between access opportunities to the tertiary system and inclusion in different socioeconomic strata, which shows the difficulties faced by least-income sectors to access higher education. As demonstrated in Figure 4.1, the countries that show a higher degree of inequity in access, taking into account family socioeconomic status, are Bolivia, Brazil, Honduras, Uruguay, Peru, and Mexico, where less than 5 percent of the population between 18 and 24 years old belongs to the poorest quintile (Q1) of access to higher education. In contrast, countries where there is a greater participation of young people from the richest quintile (Q5) are Colombia, Costa Rica, and Chile. In all Latin American countries, the wealthiest strata are overrepresented within the higher education system.

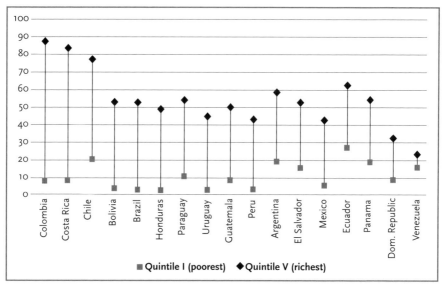

Source: CINDA (2011).

Equity in Relation to Outcomes
In order to analyze equity in relation to outcomes, three relevant indicators will be reviewed: (1) Annual number of higher education graduates by gender, (2) open unemployment rate for people with 13 or more years of education, and (3) efficiency of graduation according to gender.

Figure 4.2 demonstrates how women have continued gaining ground compared to men. This is explained by their increasing entrance into higher education and the workforce. In that sense, professional certification is becoming more valued by women, who outnumber men in most of the studied countries. The only exceptions to this trend are Colombia and Cuba, where the relationship between men and women tertiary graduates is still favorable to the former. This phenomenon was unthinkable 20 or 30 years ago when the predominance of men within the system and, consequently, the subsequent graduation rate of this group were much higher than women's.

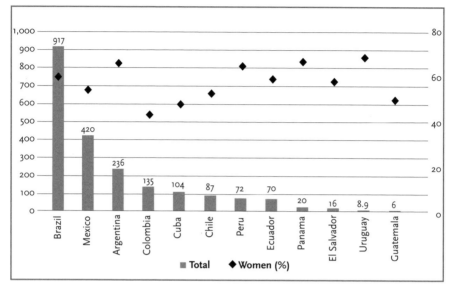

Source: CINDA (2011).

As indicated, a proxy indicator will be used to evaluate what has happened in the area of equity in relation to outcomes. For this, the open unemployment rate for people with 13 or more years of education is a useful parameter, because it is possible to discern whether there has been some progress in the population with some level of higher education in terms of employability. The data in Table 4.3 show that in the last decade the employability rates of the population with tertiary studies has improved in countries like Argentina, Bolivia, Colombia, Panama, and Peru. In contrast, in countries like Brazil, Chile, Ecuador, and El Salvador, the opposite has occurred (see Table 4.3).

TABLE 4.3: Open unemployment rate in the population with 13 or more years of education (1990, 2002, and 2009)

Countries	1990	2002	2009
Argentina	3	14.3	6.6
Bolivia	8.1	6.6	...
Brazil	1.8	4.8	5
Chile	6.3	6.7	8.6
Colombia	7.3	14	11.5
Costa Rica	2.8	3.2	3.2
Ecuador	6.1	7.3	8.5
El Salvador	...	4.5	6.5
Guatemala	2.1	6	...
Honduras	6	5.7	...
Mexico	2.3	4.6	...
Panama	15.2	13	6.5
Paraguay	3.7	6.8	6.9
Peru	...	6.4	5.3
Dominican Republic	...	7.5	5.8
Uruguay	5.9	12.2	4.5
Venezuela	6.1	15.7	...

Source: CINDA (2011).

Finally, the graduation efficiency rate of higher education is a good proxy indicator for sizing the equity of outcomes phenomenon. The numbers in Table 4.4 reveal that women take less time to graduate than men. Indeed, with the exception of Guatemala, a higher proportion of women graduate from the system, which could be partly explained by the greater time commitment that they make to study.

TABLE 4.4: GRADUATION EFFICIENCY IN HIGHER EDUCATION IN LATIN AMERICA: FIVE-YEAR AVERAGES (2001–2005) (%)

Countries	Men	Women	Total
Bolivia	...	...	15.0
Brazil	52.6	67.0	60.7
Chile	43.4	49.6	46.3
Costa Rica	...	...	46.0
Colombia	69.3	79.8	74.4
Cuba	74.4	75.2	75.0
Guatemala	15.8	8.4	24.4
Paraguay	58.0	75.0	67.0
Uruguay	28.0	28.0	28.0
Venezuela	40.0	57.9	48.0

Source: CINDA (2007).

Conclusion

Latin American countries have experienced a significant increase in higher education enrollment and coverage for the 18–24 age group. This increase has resulted in a partial democratization of access, since these rising numbers also reflect in the increase of the population (quintile 1 and women) that, historically and proportionally, have had the lowest participation in terms of access to the tertiary education system.

The rising access to higher education in Latin America can be attributed in part to a sustained increase in private sector offerings. Currently about half of the enrollment at the undergraduate level is concentrated in the private sector. However, this implies greater inequity, since the education offered in these institutions is paid by the families and the students themselves. Consequently, the increase in enrollment and coverage in recent years has not necessarily ensured equity of access. In fact, the participation of young people from the most vulnerable sectors in society is still far from that of young people from the wealthiest strata. The inequality described here may in part be remedied by the creation of a state policy supported by investment according to the needs of the countries to ensure the entry of the most deserving students and the students with least resources through various means of financing, including scholarship programs, state credits, and/or total exemption of fees. However, these funding mechanisms do not guarantee the quality of the provided service or the subsequent insertion into the workplace. When the state intervenes in market mechanisms, these measures must be accompanied by work-monitoring systems and systems of quality accreditation of the provided services.

Chile has also experienced these processes. Despite the achievements in access and coverage (increase in scholarships and credits, increase in coverage by income quintile, and the inclusion of ethnic minorities), there is awareness among different actors that it is necessary to promote actions and initiatives aimed at improving the quality of education offered at all levels.

The compiled data show that existing gaps in access and survival must be reduced. One of the remaining tasks involves improving economic assistance to young people who attend (or wish to take) technical studies (mostly associated to the poorest quintiles), which to date do not yet have enough support to fund their education.

In terms of the results calculated in this chapter from proxy indicators such as graduation rates by gender at the undergraduate level and the unemployment rate for people with 13 or more years of schooling, it is possible to conclude that there has been a significant advance in women's participation in higher education, which has resulted in graduation rates that exceed those of men at the regional level. This progress, however, is not necessarily associated with a set of state-promoted policies or strategies but rather with the desire of women to attain professional certification that allows them to have autonomy and greater possibilities of personal and professional development. In addition, unemployment rates in the population with higher education (not necessarily completed) have decreased in several countries of the region. In these cases, the signs are not categorical and therefore do not allow us to extract clear conclusions. This occurs to a large degree because of the oscillations of the economy in the last 20 years. Moreover, there is no state policy or strategy designed to favor the employment of people with tertiary studies.

In light of the results already discussed and the policies/strategies driven by governments and higher education institutions, it is conceivable that in the coming years there will be significant improvements both in access and rate of retention and in the area of outcomes (higher levels of employment and better salaries for graduates of the system), which jeopardize the logic of social and culture reproduction that has prevailed to this day in the third world.

NOTES

[1] There are, of course, other features associated with equity, such as retention, achievement, outcomes and employability (Latorre, González, & Espinoza, 2009).

REFERENCES

Berner, B. (2002). "Kunskapssamhällets" paradoxer: utbildningens betydelser ochkönsrelationernas roll [The knowledge society's paradoxes: The importance of education and the roll of gender relations]. In Lennart Sturesson et al. (Eds.), *Spänningsfält: Tekniken, Politiken, Framtiden*. Stockholm, Sweden: Carlsson.

Carlson, K. (1983). How equal is equal? *Journal of Educational Equity and Leadership, 3*(3), 243–257.

CINDA. (2007). *Educación Superior en Ibero América: Informe 2007*. Chile, Centro Interuniversitario de Desarrollo (CINDA). Retrieved from http://www.cinda.org

CINDA. (2011). *Educación superior en Iberoamérica. Informe 2011*. Santiago, Chile: Ril Editores.

Corson, D. (2001). Ontario students as a means to a government's ends. *Our Schools/Our Selves, 10*(4), 55–77.

Deutsch, M. (1975). Equity, equality, and need: What determines which value will be used as the basis of distributive justice? *Journal of Social Issues, 31*(3), 137–149.

Espinoza, O. (2002). *The global and national rhetoric of educational reform and the practice of (in) equity in access to the Chilean higher education system, 1981–1998* (Doctoral dissertation, School of Education, University of Pittsburgh).

Espinoza, O. (2007). Solving the equity/equality conceptual dilemma: A new model for analysis of the educational process. *Educational Research, 49*(4), 343–363.

Espinoza, O., González, L. E., & Castillo, D. (2007). *Estudio analítico comparativo del sistema educacional de MERCOSUR: Educación superior*. Brasilia, Brazil: PNUD-MEC/INEP.

Evans, P. (2004). Educating students with special needs: A comparison of inclusion practices in OECD countries. *Education Canada, 44*(1), 32–35.

Gordon, E. W. (1972). Toward defining equality of educational opportunity. In F. Mosteller & D. Moynihan (Eds.), *On equality of educational opportunity* (pp. 423–434). New York, NY: Random House.

Harvey, G., & Klein, S. (1985). Understanding and measuring equity in education: A conceptual model. *Journal of Educational Equity and Leadership, 5*(2), 145–168.

Latorre, C. L., González, L. E., & Espinoza, O. (2009). *Equidad en educación superior: Evaluación de las políticas públicas de la concertación*. Santiago, Chile: Editorial Catalonia/Fundación Equitas.

Lerner, M. (1974). The justice motive: "Equity" and "parity" among children. *Journal of Personality and Social Psychology, 29*(4), 539–550.

Malatest, R. (2004). *Aboriginal peoples and post-secondary education: What educators have learned* (Report). Montreal, Canada: R.A. Malatest & Associates Ltd. for the Canada Millennium Scholarship Foundation. Retrieved from http://www.turtleisland.org/education/postseced.pdf

Martin, L. (1994). *Equity and general performance indicators in higher education: Vol. 1. Equity indicators*. Canberra, Australia: AGPS.

Martins, S., Mauritti, R., & Costa, A. (2005). *Condições socioeconómicas dos estudantes do ensino superior em Portugal*. Lisbon, Portugal: Direcção Geral do Ensino Superior.

OECD. (2004a). *Learning for tomorrow's world: First results from PISA 2003*. Paris, France: OECD.

OECD. (2004b). *Career guidance and public policy: Bridging the gap*. Paris, France: OECD.

OECD. (2007a). *No More Failures: Ten Steps to Equity in Education*. Paris, France: OECD.

OECD. (2007b). *Education at a glance: OECD indicators 2007*. Paris, France: OECD.

OECD. (2008). *Tertiary education for the knowledge society.* Paris, France: OECD.

Secada, W. (1989). Educational equity versus equality of education: An alternative conception. In W. Secada (Ed.), *Equity and education* (pp. 68–88). New York, NY: Falmer.

Tumin, M. (1965). *The meaning of equality in education.* Paper presented at the Third Annual Conference of the National Committee for support of Public Schools. Washington, DC.

Warner, W., Havighurst, R., & Loeb, M. (1944). Who shall be educated? In W. Warner, R. Havighurst, & M. Loeb, *Who shall be educated? The challenge of unequal opportunities* (pp. 141–172). New York, NY: Harper.

Chapter Five

Trends in Student and Academic Mobility in Latin America: From "Brain Drain" to "Brain Gain"

Sylvie Didou Aupetit, Cinvestav, National Polytechnic Institute, Mexico

In Latin America, the concepts of regional brain drain and brain gain refer to the outgoing and incoming flow of students, graduates, and professionals. In general, the data show that more citizens are emigrating than returning, and that highly qualified foreign immigrants are living in the region. To various extents, scopes, and levels of quality, the data describe the trend's direction, size, and characteristics based on measurements that are difficult to compare.[1] They are of little use for quantifying foreign student enrollments in Latin American countries or academic and scientific faculty members who, regardless of their national origin, have achieved their highest level of schooling in another country.

This situation presents challenges to institutions of higher education and to governments, because the information available to them is inadequate for evaluating and making decisions regarding mobility programs, supporting equality policies, and improving the quality and review of regulations and models of organization and action on exchanges.

To account for this, and despite current changes, let's consider the assertion that student and academic mobility contribute little to building innovative institutions, diversifying instruction, redistributing opportunities, developing neosocial elites to stabilize and sustain Latin American societies, and integrating them into a regional geopolitical bloc. To prove this hypothesis, we will examine the dynamics of mobility from the standpoint of brain drain and brain gain and provide examples of enlightening practices. We will also identify what is needed for public action and research, concluding with suggestions of ways to strengthen these ties with capacity-building processes, tactical positions with respect to globalization, and proposals for cooperation toward progress.

Student Mobility: Between Tradition and Rearticulation

During the first decade of the 21st century, student mobility in Latin America was below the world average in terms of spatial displacement, regardless of education level or direction of movement. In 2009, a total of 195,951 students moved to another country, representing approximately 1 percent of total regional enrollments and 5.8 percent of international student enrollments worldwide. Of those students, 52.6 percent came from Mexico, Brazil, Colombia, Peru, and Venezuela, in descending order. Their main destinations were to North America and Western Europe, accounting for 73.3 percent of Latin American and Caribbean mobility, compared to 58.6 percent overall (UNESCO Institute for Statistics [UIS], 2011). Structurally, fewer mobile Latin American students are enrolled in graduate programs compared to other groups (Motivans, 2009), with the exception of Brazilians and Colombians.

The flow of incoming and outgoing students is unbalanced in terms of number and origin. In 2009, 80,271 foreign students moved to Latin American countries, of which 55.8 percent came from the same region. However, the data are incomplete. Only Anguilla, Barbuda, Aruba, Barbados, Bermuda, Brazil, Chile, Costa Rica, Cuba, El Salvador, Granada, Guyana, the Cayman Islands, the British Virgin Islands, Saint Lucia, and Venezuela reported information on their foreign students (UIS, 2011). Argentina and Mexico both have this information, but did not submit it to UNESCO (Didou, Duriez, Luchilo, Piscoya, & Stubrin, 2012).

Regionally, international mobility is governed by run-of-the-mill organizational arrangements and national or institutional regulations that hinder their growth and connections with transformative policies on higher education. Due to protectionism, or power struggles between competing voices and interests within universities, many countries have done little to expand mobility. They have increased the number of programs supporting student mobility, but in an improvised and disjointed manner, thereby limiting their effects to a small number of beneficiaries. They are no closer to resolving one of the biggest obstacles to strengthening extra–Ibero American mobility, namely, poor levels of learning English and other foreign languages in public schools. There are more mobility programs available, but potential applicants lack the language skills required to leave their own culture, which results in many scholarships going unawarded.

Despite these limitations, there are some clear changes in how student mobility is being structured and in its social-assigned value. The first change is related to the increased popularity of short-term stays supported by mediocre offers. The appeal is further eroded by delays and difficulties in approving courses completed in outside institutions.

Another change is the diversification of groups according to national priority. Though Nicaragua and Guatemala, with their lack of postgraduate programs, focus their programs on the teaching and research faculty, other countries tweak their mobility opportunities to benefit those in need (indigenous people, people of African descent, immigrants, and the poor) in cooperation with international organizations or bilateral cooperation agencies. Canada's Emerging Leaders in the Americas program, which started in 2009 for 39 countries throughout Latin America and the Caribbean, provides funding for short stays in Canada for undergraduate and graduate students who exhibit social leadership skills.[2] From 2001 to 2013, the Ford Foundation International Fellowships Program granted national and international scholarships to graduate students from Brazil, Chile, Guatemala, Mexico, and Peru in order to reverse the inequities they faced in accessing and completing their higher education. These opportunities reflect an emerging interest in high-level student mobility programs that do not exclusively target privileged students, but rather students who have struggled against inequality.

A third significant change relates to the inclusion of international student mobility in institutional and program positions, in order to guarantee shared responsibilities among candidates and other institutional members in achieving results. In Mexico, the National Science and Technology Council (CONACYT) defines the conditions for granting temporary mobility scholarships (mixed scholarships) based on past cooperation between the scientific teams in the source and target countries, the applicant's enrollment in an accredited graduate program, and the applicant's involvement in research projects. Not only is the beneficiary in compliance with his or her graduation and return requirements, but his or her stay also develops a connection between individual or group processes in order to build skills, develop research, improve career opportunities, and strengthen institutional resources.

A fourth change is rooted in strengthening subregional poles for nearby inbound and outbound mobility in Chile, Cuba, Costa Rica, and (to a lesser extent) Mexico, given the deliberate promotion of their instruction (via consulates, exchange agreements, graduate program fairs) and their social (safety, cost of living, etc.) and educational (quality, cost, etc.) benefits. The most pronounced (yet unusual) demonstration of rapidly expanding inbound mobility and spatial redeployment is Cuba, where the number of foreign students who immigrated went from 3,740 in 1999 to 30,961 in 2009. During that time, the African contingent went from accounting for 67.4 to 7.9 percent of the respective totals, while Latin Americans (mainly Bolivians, Venezuelans, Ecuadorians, Peruvians, Mexicans, Argentines, Brazilians, Central Americans, and Caribbeans) increased their involvement from 6.7 to 54.3 percent (UIS, 2011, pp. 173–182). These shifts are symptomatic of the partial displacement of proactive internationalization processes to North America and Europe in exchange for other Spanish-language internationalization processes, based on the abilities of individual students, the role of Spanish and Latin American university associations and networks, and the support of various governments for cultural and diplomatic integration policies. They also highlight volatile combinations (to be monitored) of mobility programs in nearby areas with other cultural, linguistic, or otherwise prestigious programs, revealing distortions between what is intended and what actually occurs.

Despite these changes, the regional and national statistics on international student mobility have not improved. The Map of Higher Education, sponsored by the International Institute for Higher Education in Latin America and the Caribbean (IESALC) since 2007, has faltered. Progress has been slow on national registers of inbound mobility. The National Survey of Mexico's International Student Mobility, conducted by the Mexican Secretariat of Public Education in 2011, has had low response rates on its questionnaire (22.5 percent of the 505 institutions that were contacted). As a result, the available information is used to evaluate quantitative results (scholarship programs; see Luchilo, 2010; Mazza, 2009) more than to analyze new topics. While French researchers are interested in how to incorporate foreign students (Campus France, 2010; Agulhon & Xavier de Brito, 2009; Enafaa & Paivandi, 2008) and the implications of their mobility in the transfer from theory-based schools (García & Muñoz, 2009), Latin Americans ignore these aspects, even when they can boost the international visibility for their opportunities for higher education, increase demand, and lower mobile student dropout rates.

In short, characterizing student mobility in, to, and from Latin America and reviewing the knowledge we have about it confirm that the region is in a state of transition. This leads to the conclusion that categorically differentiating beneficiaries (*free movers,* academics, members of vulnerable groups, and their heirs) should be linked to more diversified programs, application selection procedures, mobility preparation mechanisms, and support in the destination country. To do this, it would be necessary to get information from enrollment registers on mobility. In addition to being a precursor for individual integration into conventional elites or budding teachers, scientists, or intellectuals, is mobility essential for integrating innovative niches of academic professionalization (research areas, disciplinary areas)? Is it linked to how transnationalized sectors operate (in the areas of health care in Monterrey, Mexico, and Medellin, Colombia)?

With data such as these, it would be feasible to restructure student mobility programs in order to strengthen their ties with internationalization policies (in which they are key components) and with projects to consolidate various institutions of higher learning (Rama, 2011). Going beyond the primary dynamic of responding to casual opportunities would also involve improving the effective operation of junior researchers and alumni networks in order to share resources and information for starting professional careers in less unfavorable conditions than what can be found in the region's institutions and helping to develop a more favorable location in globalized scenarios.

Academic Mobility and Internationalization of Scientific Fields in Latin America

For many years the governing bodies of higher education and scientific research in the region's developing countries supported short- and long-length stays, sabbaticals, and seminars outside of their academics, whether self-funded or in cooperation with approved international cooperation organizations (Martin-Sempere, Rey, & Plaza, 1999). In the late 1990s, academic mobility returned the focus to graduate students in order to improve the poor school accommodations of the teaching and scientific faculty (Veras Godoy, 2010). Between 1998 and 2010, Mexico's Teachers Improvement Program granted 2,329 scholarships to master's and doctoral level foreigners and reported 1,200 degrees.

In the past decade, Argentina, Mexico, and other countries have set up bilateral disciplinary networks as additional measures to enable scientific mobility to contribute to building endogenous abilities and improve teaching and research. They organized shared careers or cograduation, with study abroad requirements for students and/or academics. They signed bilateral or interinstitutional agreements for sandwich stays, completing doctoral studies abroad, and ongoing professional career development opportunities for researchers.

It is easy to illustrate the successive steps of public policies for academic mobility. It isn't about calibrating transformative power. Experts stress the historical role of public policy in reproducing and expanding Latin America's intellectual elite and in the national approach to assigning prestige to globalized scientific systems (Didou & Gérard, 2010), but it is difficult to assess the repercussions in the internal and external organization and prioritization of systems and institutions and in the transfer of knowledge. Regarding inbound scientific mobility, although they warned that immigrants affect the habits of its existing groups, its international connections, and its lines and forms of work (for Mexico, see Izquierdo, 2008; for Brazil, see Mazza, 2009), many Latin American countries do not count how many are institutional or program mechanisms, except in certain cases. In 2009, 2,167 of the 15,561 prestigious academics grouped in Mexico's National System of Researchers were born outside of the country. More than a third (833) came from Latin America; 243, from Spain; 197, the United States; 177, Argentina; and 155, the Russian Federation. These data show a pattern of movement for both people and knowledge in the Spanish-speaking world (including Spain) and its disassociation from the teaching of repatriated citizens, who are mainly graduates students in US and European epicenters of student mobility (Didou & Gérard, 2010). Despite the relevance of such comparisons in redefining the paths of scientific mobility and international cooperative strategies, there are no comparable indicators on a regional level concerning the results of programs (such as the incorporation of young Spanish doctoral students in Latin American universities on behalf of the Spanish Agency for International Development Cooperation) or consistent statistics on scientific immigration to Latin America. Only information on national programs (Cátedras Patrimoniales of Excellence II for foreign researchers under CONACYT in Mexico) is available, making it impossible, with these sources, to account for the complexity of reverse academic mobility guidelines on a regional level. Discussion, therefore, refers to formal support mechanisms more than to monitoring the adequacy of investments or meeting objectives. In general, this ignores how many Latin American graduate students living abroad are established in the academic markets of the countries where they studied and how many are in their original countries. The success of reinsertion programs for scientists returning to national institutions is mentioned, regardless of the wasted human potential that sometimes may occur (for Brazil, see Balbachevsky & Marques, 2009).

In conclusion, detecting the exchange routes for researchers and knowledge is an imperfect science, both nationally and regionally, despite the reconceptualization of academic mobility as a two-way process, from inside to outside and from outside to inside, and the implementation of proactive programs for inviting foreigners or repatriates (e.g., *Prometeo Viejos Sabios*, in 2010, by the Inter-American Development Bank [IDB] and the government of Ecuador). To compensate for what is missing, we need to analyze the impacts of academic mobility on the legitimization of innovative institutions with supranational aspects or Latin American integration (e.g., Federal University of Latin American Integration in Brazil) to test pilot associations between centers (e.g., scientific observatories such as the Cousteau Observatory in Costa Rica, supported by France and Mexico; or French–Mexican disciplinary colleges for social sciences). It is important to evaluate how multilateral, international, governmental, associative, and civil organizations stimulate international scientific mobility, in coordination with preferred partners, and how these downward and upward trends are supervised, considering the juxtapositions between countries that reduce their support and others who expand it (for Brazil, see Knobel, 2012).

Estimates of Brain Drain and Realities of Brain Gain

Responses to brain drain (since the 1950s in Argentina, see Oteiza, 1970) have been based on information provided by national statistics offices, specialized regional (the Latin American Demographic Center [CELADE]) or international organizations interested in highly qualified mobility (e.g., Continuous Reporting System on Migration–Organisation for Economic Co-operation and Development [SOPEMI-OECD]), and experts in source and target countries.

Starting 10 years ago, a renewal of interest among decision-makers and researchers in evaluating talent circulation and ability loss throughout most of the region led to the publication of various qualitative and quantitative analyses. These analyses vary in scope, due to the uneven and disorderly accumulation of materials. Knowledge is inconsistent, and it fails to reflect the diversity of national situations. In the early 2000s, expatriation rates for highly skilled individuals were 8.8 percent across Latin America (Dumont, Spielvogel, & Widmaier, 2010), exceeding the World Bank's "critical" threshold (Ermolieva, 2011) of 10 percent in Belize, Cuba, the Dominican Republic, Nicaragua, Panama, El Salvador, and Uruguay. Paradoxically, the countries with lower expatriation rates (Brazil, 2.6 percent; Peru, 5 percent; Mexico, 5.4 percent; and Venezuela, Argentina, and Colombia, 6.3 percent) provided the most consistent information on the migration of highly qualified individuals (SOPEMI-OECD, 2011). The proportion of people with doctoral degrees who obtained their degrees in their original countries compared to the United States was 43 percent for Argentines in 2003 and 2.5 percent for Brazilians in 2005 (Luchilo & Stubrin, 2011). In 2009, approximately 20 percent of Mexico-born individuals with a doctoral degree were living in the United States (compared to an average of 11 percent), and the number of people with doctoral degrees in Mexico's National System of Researchers was less than the number of Mexicans with doctoral degrees living in the United States (16,000 and 20,000, respectively) (BBVA Research, 2010). With regard to intentions of remaining in the country of graduation, "the percentage of Mexican doctoral students planning to stay in the United States once they have completed their studies is similar to that of Brazil and substantially less than that of Argentina, Colombia, and Peru" and those with "plans and firm plans to remain in the United States grew between 1994–95 and 2002–05, from 40.2% to 46.6% with plans and from 21.5% to 31.5% with firm plans" (CONACYT, 2011, p. 146). We also have disparate knowledge of expatriates, broken down by education, target country, related programs, courses, terms for entering/exiting the workforce, and intentions of returning.

Public policies on academic markets in Latin America essentially aim to discourage the exodus of the most qualified individuals and to encourage their return. Some have even tried to control outbound mobility and increase retention. In Mexico, CONACYT restricted the number of international scholarships on the pretext of having a domestic supply of accredited postgraduates, and measures were implemented for keeping young individuals with doctoral degrees in the country. Brazil and Cuba increased the penalties applied to scholarships in the event that the recipient emigrates or does not graduate. Other countries encouraged the repatriation of their citizens living abroad. In the 1980s, such programs were highly political, cropping up as nations reconciled after a conflict. After the demise of their military dictatorships, Argentina, Brazil, Chile, and Uruguay implemented measures to encourage exiled citizens to return, through joint ventures among national governments, foreign international cooperation agencies, university associations, and bilateral and international organizations, such as UNESCO and the International Organization for Migration (IOM). They later expanded geographically and to other beneficiaries. Colombia, Ecuador, El Salvador, Jamaica, Mexico, and Peru used government, association, or international funds to support the return of their citizens with doctoral degrees who were working for foreign institutions of higher education and research and put them into contact with potential employers. Most of these initiatives, however, produced only limited results due to inadequate resources, difficulty in identifying beneficiaries, and unsatisfactory placements in agencies.

To adjust their return programs, Argentina, Chile, Honduras, Uruguay, and Venezuela conducted a census of their communities abroad, with an emphasis on those with higher education. In 2003, Argentina found that its scientists and engineers living abroad represented approximately 10 percent of the country's total population and 26 percent of the total number of people employed in science and technology (Luchilo & Stubrin, 2011).

In the past decade, with the success of the "intellectual diaspora" concept, promoted by the World Bank and others, a large number of countries in Latin America (17 according to a regional survey; see Organización Internacional para las Migraciones, 2005) had implemented programs to (re)connect with its scientists (in person or online). Such programs include the Network of Argentine Researchers and Scientists Living Abroad, Chile Global, Salvadoreños Afuera, Colombia Nos Une, Caldas Colombian Network of Scientists and Engineers Abroad, Peruvian Science Network, and the Network of Mexican Talent Abroad (López Chatelt, 2009). El Salvador, Mexico, Argentina, Chile, and Uruguay have organized joint talent banks to showcase short-term cooperation opportunities on products of mutual interest. After a period during which diaspora programs built enthusiasm (see the project to create knowledge incubators among Argentina, Colombia, France, and Uruguay[3]), the IOM, IDB, and other migration-tracking organizations warned that they were not miracle solutions (Agunias, 2009). Although this was likely to create interactions among disciplinary groups, build the talents of the weaker partners, pool equipment for research, diversify careers, and develop cooperation in preferred student mobility projects, there were also some disadvantages. For instance, they were rooted in the weak connections among the temporary reverse migration, return, and diaspora programs, and the criteria for selecting partners among the many foreign-based Latin American associations was unclear. Finally, there was little transparency with regard to supplies and products, performance objectives, and results.

Regional and national organizations have recently set up systems to support and generate information in order to better understand scientific migrations and to identify duplicate practices. In 2010, UNESCO's IESALC established the Observatory on Academic and Scientific Mobility as a theme-national unit system for Argentina (headquartered at the University of Cuyo in Mendoza), Colombia (in the Association of Colombian Universities [ASCUN]), and Panama (in the University of Panama).[4]

Despite these efforts, the emerging economies of Latin America have inadequate mechanisms, given the brain drain, to sustain strategic and focused brain gain programs designed to improve the quality and equality of higher education and research systems. Although the region's governments have recognized that reversing the disadvantages brought about by brain drain and increasing reverse migration were part of their positioning to UNESCO at the Regional and World Conferences on Higher Education (in Colombia in June 2008 and in Paris in July 2009), specific initiatives have progressed parsimoniously, and operating the portal for the Higher Education Networks of Latin America and the Caribbean, mainly for international academic cooperation, is not entirely reliable.

Conclusions: Suggestions for Action Items and Further Research

Over the past decade in Latin America, international student mobility, as well as brain drain and brain gain with respect to systems for higher education and science, have sparked interest and gained sectoral relevance. However, they have been analyzed based on inconsistent documented studies. Correcting this situation requires that researchers and experts pay attention to unknown aspects of both phenomena using comprehensive approaches and that decision makers revise their policies.

Research Agenda
One perspective to include in a regional research agenda is a comparison model. This would provide regional or subregional views of the flow of students and scientists, develop typologies of situations based on common approaches and scales, and identify who is directly or indirectly affected by brain drain and who is committed to reversing it. For these purposes, it would be necessary to agree on research priorities for brain gain strategies to improve the quality of services and the social responsibilities of institutions. Bilateral or multilateral projects should be set up in order to establish complex and differentiated paths of international mobility and the intermediary roles

played by highly qualified migrants and students. The characteristics of mobility change quickly depending on contextual factors (recession and growth cycles), and therefore policy decisions on migration, employment, and science, specific research must be encouraged on mutual topics, such as linking changes in programs supporting international mobility and economic and social crises.

Policy Agenda
When considering who should fund international mobility, under what guidelines, and for what purposes, policies should focus on the rationalization, expansion, focus, and visibility of mobility offers. To avoid duplicating programs, and to specify profiles, create opportunities, reduce wasted scholarships, and justify the channeling of significant resources, it is important to build national- and regional-scale mechanisms for unifying information and directing it to those who are interested. Next, the priorities should be ranked, and benefit groups among university players and establishments should be prioritized. Existing exchange flows must be reinforced. With this approach, professional portals to attract foreign scientists in key areas will be encouraged, by combining internationalization and mobility programs for innovation and excellence.

On an institutional level, mobility within institutional consolidation would be evaluated from the standpoint of providing high-quality teaching and research services with greater coverage. Beyond the self-satisfied rhetoric about its benefits (questioned today by internationalization advocates; see Knight, 2011; Brandenburg & de Wit, 2011), it is important to monitor whether restructuring processes are being developed in establishments instead of discretionally favoring individual mobility. The latter would mean that establishments are producing strategic plans to promote mobility within the sector, with performance indicators, and that they are making the necessary investments in order to achieve objectives. The likelihood of getting results and making performance transparent depends on effective management, professional training, and cooperation. All gray areas must be dispelled because they hinder the understanding of how internationalization processes actually work, and they jeopardize the stability of these processes.

Pending Issues
Regardless of the various stages of mobility development in Latin American countries, both ends of mobility programs have readjusted their connections based on a redefinition of mutual expectations and interests. For example, Spain assigned special attention to Colombia, Costa Rica, Cuba, the Dominican Republic, Ecuador, Guatemala, Honduras, Nicaragua, Paraguay, and El Salvador. In addition, the demand for educating academics and doctoral students through foreign institutions is shifting, depending on the level of consolidation of national education systems at this level. In 2009, Brazil, Mexico, and Argentina graduated 11,368, 2,714, and 937 of the

15,249 enrollments in doctoral programs, while Ecuador, Guatemala, Paraguay, El Salvador, Uruguay, and Venezuela produced fewer than 100 doctoral students each year. A change in demand is expected. The number of international mobility applications will increase in countries with inadequate authority given to teachers and researchers, but some students will move to Brazil or Mexico. Meanwhile, people leaving countries with strong national postgraduate systems will be more specific in terms of their areas of specialization, and they will prefer to be linked with accredited institutions outside of the region.

Another issue that will generate increased discussion is the matter of who will pay for student and scientific mobility. Regional offerings are structured into business and support programs, but we do not know how they are internally balanced. In Latin America, where the poverty rate is over 33 percent and one out of every eight people is living in extreme poverty (Puryear & Jewers, 2009), the privatization of mobility programs and awarding of money to beneficiaries must be carefully supervised. One last topic that should be included in a discussion on the future of mobility is the best combinations of virtual exchanges and physical movements of individuals in order to keep costs down while also guaranteeing effectiveness and usefulness.

NOTES

[1] Brain drain is typically measured by expatriation, professional retention, and graduation rates. These measurements may indicate how many graduates are working in the country or abroad, how many have been awarded the same degree in a given year, or how many have left the country where they studied. The proportion of emigrants increases as their degree level increases and decreases over time.

[2] See the official website at http://www.scholarships-bourses.gc.ca/scholarships-bourses/can/institutions/elap

[3] See http://issuu.com/observatoriodiasporas/docs/proyectocidesal/1?mode=a_p

[4] See "Sobre el Observatorio de Movilidades Académicas y Científicas," http://www.iesalc.unesco.org.ve/index.php?option=com_content&view=article&id=1813:sobre-obsmac&catid=194&Itemid=746

REFERENCES

Agulhon, C., & Xavier de Brito, A. (2009). *Les étudiants étrangers à Paris: entre affiliation et repli.* Paris, France: L'Harmattan.

Agunias, D. (Ed.). (2009). *Foreword, closing the distance: How governments strengthen ties with their diasporas.* Washington, DC: Migration Policy Institute.

Balbachevsky, E., & Marques, F. (2009). "Fuga de cerebros" en Brasil: Los costos públicos de un errado entendimiento de una realidad académica" In S. Didou Aupetit & E. Gérard (Eds.), *Fuga de cerebros, movilidad académica y redes científicas. Perspectivas latinoamericanas* (pp. 181–173). Mexico City, Mexico: IESALC–CINVESTAV– IRD. Retrieved from http://unesdoc.unesco.org/images/0018/001864/186433s.pdf

BBVA Research, (2010). México, situación migración. Mexico City, Mexico: BBVA-Bancomer. Retrieved from http://www.bbvaresearch.com/KETD/fbin/mult/1011_SitMigracionMexico_04_tcm346–234630.pdf?ts=12112010

Brandenburg, U., & de Wit, H. (2011). "The end of internationalization." *International Higher Education, 62*, 15–16.

Campus France. (2010). Les notes de Campus France, no. 26, octobre. *La mobilité des étudiants d'Amérique Latine.* Paris, France: Author.

CONACYT. (2011). *Evaluación de impacto del programa de formación de científicos y tecnólogos 1997–2006.* Mexico City, Mexico: CONACYT.

Didou S., Duriez, M., Luchilo, L., Piscoya, L., & Stubrin, A. (2012). *La formación internacional de los científicos en América Latina.* Mexico City, Mexico: ANUIES-IESALC.

Didou, S., & Gérard, E. (2010). *El SNI, veinticinco años después: Entre internacionalización y distinción.* Mexico City, Mexico: ANUIES.

Dumont, J. C., Spielvogel, G., & Widmaier, S., (2010). *International migrants in developed, emerging and developing countries: An extended profile* (Social, Employment and Migration Working Paper 114). Paris, France: OECD. Retrieved from http://www.oecd.org/dataoecd/35/25/46535003.pdf

Enafaa, R., & Paivandi, S. (2008). *Les étudiants étrangers en France: Enquêtes sur les projets, les parcours et les conditions de vie.* Paris, France: Observatoire de la Vie Etudiante.

Ermolieva , E. (2011). Fuga o intercambio de talentos: Nuevas líneas de investigación. *Nueva Sociedad, 233.* Retrieved from http://www.nuso.org/upload/articulos/3778_1.pdf

García, A., & M.C. Muñoz (Ed.). (2009). Mobilité universitaire et circulation internationale des idées: Le Brésil et la mondialisation des savoirs. In *Cahiers de la recherche sur l'éducation et les savoirs,* Hors série n.2. Paris, France: ARES

Izquierdo Campos, A. I. (2008). *Los científicos extranjeros en la UNAM (1990).* COMIE, IX Congreso de Investigación Educativa, Mexico City, Mexico, Universidad Veracruzana. Retrieved from http://www.comie.org.mx/congreso/memoriaelectronica/v09/ponencias/at04/PRE1178300605.pdf

Knight, J., (2011). Five myths about internationalization. *International Higher Education, 62*, 14–15.

Knobel, M. (2012). Brazil's student mobility initiative. *International Higher Education, 66*, 15–16.

López Chatelt, P. A. (2009). *Diáspora calificada mexicana.* 69 Jornada informativa de la Red de Talentos. Mexico City, Mexico: OIM-SRE. Retrieved from http://www.redtalentos.gob.mx/images/69/pres/69oim.pdf

Luchilo, L., (2010, June 24). *Las políticas de apoyo a la formación de posgrado en América Latina: Tendencias y problemas. Evaluando resultados de los Programas de Apoyo a Becas de posgrado.* Foro internacional. Mexico City, Mexico: CONACYT-AMC

Luchilo L., & Stubrin, A. (2011). Reporte nacional sobre movilidades científicas y redes de transferencia de saberes en América Latina: Argentina. Venezuela, IESALC/OBSMAC

Martin-Sempere, C., Rey, J., & Plaza, L. (1999). Movilidad temporal de investigadores y cooperación científica internacional: Las estancias de los sabáticos latinoamericanos en España. *Interciencia*, 24(2), 107–112. Retrieved from http://www.interciencia.org/v24_02/sempere.pdf

Mazza, D., (2009). Intercambios acadêmicos internacionais: Bolsas CAPES, Cnpq y Fapesp. *Cadernos de Pesquisa, 39*(137), 521–547.

Motivans, A., (2009, July). *Tendencias mundiales en la movilidad estudiantil.* Paris, France: UNESCO. Retrieved from http://portal.unesco.org/education/es/ev.php-URL_ID=59341&URL_DO=DO_TOPIC&URL_SECTION=201.html

Organización Internacional para las Migraciones. (2005). *Diásporas como agente para el desarrollo en América Latina.* Geneva, Switzerland: Author. Retrieved from http://www.iom.int/jahia/webdav/site/myjahiasite/shared/shared/mainsite/media/docs/news/4diaspora_desarrollo.pdf

Oteiza, E. (1970). La emigración de personal altamente calificado de la Argentina. Un caso de "brain drain" latinoamericano. In J. Marsal (Ed.), *El intelectual latinoamericano. Un simposio sobre sociología de los intelectuales.* Buenos Aires, Venezuela: Editorial del Instituto.

Ozden, C., & Schiff, M. (Eds.). (2005). *International remittances and brain drain.* New York: NY, Palgrave Macmillan.

Puryear, J., & Jewers, M. M. (2009). *Pobreza y desigualdad en América Latina.* Washington, DC: The Inter-American Dialogue.

Rama, C. (2011). *Mapa de rutas para la internacionalización de la educación superior en América Latina.* Caracas, Venezuela: UCAB. Retrieved from http://www.slideshare.net/claudiorama/mapa-de-ruta-para-internacionalizarse

SOPEMI-OECD. (2011). *Emigration rates by country of origin, sex, and educational attainment levels.* Paris, France: OECD. Retrieved from http://www.oecd.org/dataoecd/31/23/46561284.pdf

UNESCO Institute for Statistics. (2011). *Global education digest: Comparing education statistics across the world.* Paris, France: UNESCO. Retrieved from http://www.uis.unesco.org/Education/Documents/ged-2011-en.pdf

Veras Godoy, H. (2010). *Internacionalización y cooperación universitaria.* Guadalajara, Mexico: II Encuentro de Rectores Universia. Retrieved from http://iycu.universiablogs.net/2010/03/08/internacionalizacion-cooperacion-universitaria/

Chapter Six

PARTNERSHIPS AND OUTPOSTS: NEW ROLES FOR U.S. UNIVERSITIES IN LATIN AMERICAN HIGHER EDUCATION

Jason E. Lane, University at Albany - SUNY

Higher education in Latin America is undergoing a rapid transformation, partly because of the increased movement of students, faculty, programs, and institutions across borders. These movements have accelerated recently because government and institutional leaders now recognize that higher education has emerged as a major form of international trade and development, and that universities in foreign countries can help achieve domestic goals (Lane & Kinser, 2011b; Lane & Owens, 2012). Moreover, institutions have been lured into the international arena by the promise of enhancing their resources and reputation (McBurnie & Ziguras, 2007; Naidoo, 2010). This combination of factors has led to a complicated mix of foreign universities and partnerships, and it has influenced the development of higher education across Latin America.

The idea that higher education crosses borders is not a new concept. For centuries, students and faculty have moved among nations in search of learning opportunities. Furthermore, no matter how tight the sanctions or how "closed" a society, it has been nearly impossible to completely restrict the transfer of knowledge across geopolitical boundaries. However, a foundational assumption about the organization of higher education has been that no matter how transient individuals and knowledge might be, institutions, and their academic programs, are domestically bound—anchored in place by a combination of the physical campus, government regulations, finances, and mission—and designed to serve the nations in which they reside. Nevertheless, over the past half-century, some colleges and universities have evolved into international actors—a result of a slow, but steady, decoupling of higher education from its home nation. The last two decades have witnessed a rapid transformation and expansion of cross-border higher education (CBHE) and the development of new forms of educational organizations and partnerships. It is now not unusual for colleges and universities to operate physical presences in multiple countries, and governments are no longer restricted to using their own public institutions to help achieve government goals (Lane & Kinser, 2011a). For example, when New York City was recently looking to create a new science and engineering–focused university within the city, it issued a call for proposals that attracted bids from around the world; the city finally settled on a partnership between Cornell University and the Israel Institute of Technology (Staley & Goldman, 2011). Any discussion of the development of higher education in Latin America needs to include examination of the partnerships and outposts that are being created by foreign education providers.

Not long ago, those studying higher education in Latin American focused mostly on the evolving tensions between the public and private sectors (Levy, 1986; Balán & de Fanelli, 1997). But the advent of CBHE has resulted in the rise of a new dichotomy in need of examination: domestic versus foreign providers of higher education. The monopoly now being challenged is that of domestic colleges and universities, with foreign institutions slowly gaining ground. For example, rather than simply providing financial support for domestic public institutions, governments in nations such as Brazil and Chile have been investing significant amounts of money to send their students away to pursue an education in a foreign institution. In addition, a handful of institutions in foreign countries have been establishing foreign educational outposts such as international branch campuses (IBCs), study abroad centers, and outreach offices in many Latin American nations. Moreover, institutions throughout Latin America are now partnering with universities in other nations on dual degree programs as well as research endeavors.

The rise of CBHE and the fall of the protections that once shored up the monopoly of domestic providers have increased the prominence of foreign education providers in serving Latin American students, building capacity in the domestic higher education marketplace, and helping Latin American governments achieve their strategic goals. The purpose of this chapter is to explore cross-border engagements in Latin America, particularly in relation to the United States. To be certain, Latin America's CBHE engagement has focused globally, though mostly on Europe and the United States (de Wit, Jaramillo, Gacel-Avila, & Knight, 2005). Focusing specifically on the United States in this chapter allows for a more in-depth examination of the particular CBHE relationships between Latin America and its northern neighbor. This focus is not meant to privilege the U.S. relationships above those that Latin American nations have with other regions of the world or to suggest that they are somehow better or different. To be certain, the focus of this chapter is on the new opportunities that exist within Latin America for those higher education institutions based outside of the region. The United States, as host to some of the most active institutions in CBHE, provides for an opportune base to explore the variety of partnerships and outposts that might exist.

The chapter examines two types of CBHE engagements: partnerships and outposts. The chapter is divided into three additional sections. The first section examines the various partnerships that exist between the United States and Latin American nations in regards to higher education. The second section analyzes the growing number of foreign educational outposts that U.S. colleges and universities are operating throughout the region. The chapter concludes with a discussion in the third section on the reasons behind the expansion of CBHE in Latin America.

Cross-Border Partnerships

The rise of CBHE has allowed for a variety of new forms of educational partnerships to emerge. Over the past decade, the term *partnership* has come to describe a wide array of bridge-building and capacity-building relationships, particularly in relation to the connections that bring together the global North and global South. USAID (1997, p. 220) suggested that North–South partnerships can make it possible to tailor development projects to local needs and concerns, thus leveraging the development of expertise of and resources of outsiders well beyond Northern capabilities. Widespread capacity building enhances the ability of Southern partners to deliver and expand their services—while reducing costs and increasing legitimacy with local governments and actors.

Of course, many partnerships that are now emerging in Latin America can no longer be construed in such a fashion. While there are still developmental efforts to build capacity in underserved and underresourced regions, many countries are becoming actively engaged in the developed world, looking for ways to harness the resources of other nations to support and achieve their strategic goals. This section examines the key actors involved in many of these existing and emerging partnerships and provides examples from the Latin American context.

The key actors in such partnerships are governments, institutions or other organizations, and individuals. The idea that governments, institutions, and individuals work together to create a higher education system is not new or noteworthy; however, consideration of partnerships within the framework of CBHE means that new arrangements become possible. This is because the governments, institutions, and individuals are no longer limited to one country; rather, these involve actors from at least two nations. As a result, the government of one country could partner with an institution in another country, or the students of one country could have their education paid for by a government of another.

Table 6.1 shows the basic forms of cross-border engagements that might exist, based on the types of primary actors involved. The shaded area shows those arrangements that are most commonly considered partnerships. For the sake of simplifying the discussion, this table assumes that there are only two nations involved and only one actor from each of those nations. Based on the matrix developed in Table 6.1, there are essentially five basic types of arrangements that might exist: (1) two governments participate in a bilateral agreement; (2) an institution in one nation partners with an institution in a different nation; (3) a government of one nation partners with the institution in another; (4) the government of one nation works directly with individuals (e.g., faculty or students) in another; and (5) the institution in one nation may work directly with an individual in another nation.

TABLE 6.1: CROSS-BORDER ENGAGEMENTS, BY ACTOR TYPE

		UNITED STATES		
		Government	Institution/Organization	Individual
LATIN AMERICAN COUNTRIES	Government	Governments enter bi- or multilateral agreements to support academic exchanges and other partnerships.	L.A. governments sponsor academic or research programs at U.S. institutions.	L.A. governments sponsor exchange programs targeted at recruiting students from the U.S.
	Institution/ Organization	U.S. government sponsors exchange programs targeted at recruiting students from the U.S.	Institutions enter into partnerships to provide degree programs or support research projects, for example.	L.A. institutions create programs to attract L.A. students or establish foreign education outposts that serve L.A. students in the United States.
	Individual	U.S. government sponsors exchange programs targeted at recruiting students from L.A. to study in the U.S.	U.S. institutions create programs to attract L.A. students or establish foreign education outposts that serve L.A. students in Latin America.	Not Applicable.

Government–Government Partnerships

The governments of Latin America are significant actors in the development of their higher education systems. For decades, public colleges and universities held a monopoly over Latin American higher education, and the private sector developed only because the public sector was unable to meet demands and the government deregulated the higher education market (Levy, 1986). Currently, governments continue to play a significant role in the development of the sector (Arocena & Sutz, 2005). This is no less true when considering CBHE; however, by its very nature, CBHE involves at least two nations and, thus, their governments (Lane & Kinser, 2011a).

Government partnerships come in several different forms, such as trade agreements, memorandums of understanding, treaties, and alliances. In terms of higher education, these partnerships tend to help facilitate the work of institutions or the movement of students. One of the earliest such attempted partnerships in Latin America was between the United States and Argentina, which signed a bilateral agreement in 1972 to support the development of science and technology, but there is no record that the agreement was actually implemented (Theiler, 2005).

More recently, the United States has entered into other partnership arrangements with Latin American countries. For example, in 2011, the U.S. National Science Foundation signed a memorandum of understanding with the Brazilian Agency for Support and Evaluation of Graduate Education. This document updated a previous scientific agreement signed in 1984 between the two nations and is intended to support collaboration between researchers in both nations and to facilitate the exchange of students between the two countries.[1] Also in 2011, the presidents of the United States and Chile affirmed a series of education-related partnerships between the two nations. These partnerships include activities that provide English-language-studies programs for Chilean citizens and support binational centers that provide information to students wanting to study in the United States.[2]

These government–government partnerships are an important component of the changing nature of higher education in Latin America. As governments in Latin America seek out partners, they expand opportunities for their institutions to move across borders, not only for those institutions partnering with foreign education providers, but also for those setting up foreign education outposts. To date, most of the flow has been for colleges and universities outside of Latin America to set up shop in Latin America, but it is likely that this will not remain unidirectional. Already, Jose Maria Vargas University, based in Venezuela, has established a campus in Florida to serve that state's Spanish-speaking population.

Government–Institution Partnerships

One of the most interesting partnerships types is that between governments and institutions. The most prominent in Latin America is the Brazil Scientific Mobility

Program sponsored by the Brazilian government. The goal of this program is to provide up to 100,000 Brazilian undergraduate students with the opportunity to pursue science, technology, engineering, and mathematics (STEM) courses at leading universities in other nations. In the United States, the Brazilian government works with the Institute for International Education (IIE) to identify qualified universities to host the students for one year of study.[3] In some cases, IIE is a primary intermediary between Brazil and the U.S. institutions; in other cases, the Brazilian government works directly with the U.S. institutions. Brazil has not been the only nation to enter into such partnerships.

In 2008, Chile and the University of California (UC) system signed an agreement to establish the Chile-California Program on Human Capital Development (Boas, 2008). This program, which builds on a decades-old relationship between Chile and the state of California, provides Chilean students with the opportunity to attend master's and doctoral programs at UC. The students' education is paid for by the Chilean Bicentennial Fund for Human Capital Development. The joint agreement also provides a framework for joint research projects between Chilean and UC scholars.

Institution–Institution Partnerships

Partnerships between institutions can take a variety of forms. Some of the most prominent are student and faculty exchanges and dual degree programs. Each partnership builds different types of cross-border relationships between the United States and Latin America. Universities throughout Latin America have established scholarly exchanges with institutions in the United States. These partnerships allow for students and faculty at one institution to spend a period of time studying and/or researching at the partner institution. For example, the University of Pennsylvania has student exchange agreements with the University of San Andres and, via the COPAConsortium, with the University of Torcuato Di Tella, the University of Salvador, and the University of Buenos Aires (Theiler, 2005). However, not all institution–institution partnerships involve solely universities. For example, Houston Community College, Jackson Community College, and Red Rocks Community College partnered with two nonprofit organizations—the National Industrial Apprenticeship Service of Brazil and the Social Service Industry of Brazil—to develop workforce training initiatives for students in both countries (Sanders, 2012).

Double degree (DD) programs are increasingly used for internationalization in Latin America (Gacel-Avila, 2009). These programs allow students to take courses at two partnering institutions and receive a degree from both institutions.[4] According to a survey by Gacel-Avila (2009), the United States was only the third most desirable partner outside of the region, with Latin American institutions preferring to partner with universities in France and Spain. The countries with the highest number of institutions engaged in DD programs are Mexico, Chile, Colombia, and Argentina. In fact, according to a survey by the Institute for International Education, Mexico was the ninth most active country in the world in terms of the number of institutions engaged in DD programs (Obst, Kuder, & Banks, 2011).

Foreign Educational Outposts

One of the results of CBHE is the development of the multinational university (MNU) (Lane & Kinser, 2011a; Kinser & Lane, 2012). MNUs exist when a college or university owns and operates a physical presence in more than one country; these presences can include branch campuses, research sites, outreach offices, and study abroad centers. The myriad forms of foreign educational outposts (FEPs) have only recently begun to capture scholarly attention; as such, theoretical examinations of such entities are mostly nonexistent. Nevertheless, many U.S. institutions operate FEPs throughout Latin America. This section provides an overview of different types of FEPs, including those currently operating in Latin America.[5]

International Branch Campus

The form of FEP that has received the most scholarly attention is the international branch campus (IBC). An IBC is "an entity that is owned, at least in part, by a foreign education provider; operated in the name of the foreign education provider; engages in at least some face-to-face teaching; and provides access to an entire academic program that leads to a credential awarded by the foreign education provider" (Lane, 2011b, p. 1). There are now nearly 200 IBCs scattered around the globe, more than half of which opened during the 2000s (C-BERT, 2012; Lawton & Katsomitros, 2012).

The United States is the largest exporter of IBCs, and most of these institutions are located in Asia and the Middle East. However, Latin America has not escaped the development of such institutions. While almost all of the known IBCs in the region are from the United States (see Table 6.2), Argentina hosts a campus of the University of Bologna in Italy, and there has been a limited amount of IBC development among nations within Latin America. For example, the University of Santa Maria in Chile operates a campus in Ecuador (C-BERT, 2012).

There are currently five U.S.-based IBCs operating in four Latin American nations. Collectively they provide evidence of the ways in which CBHE is transforming higher education, with students no longer needing to travel to the United States to pursue a U.S. degree in a campus setting. These campuses provide opportunities for local citizens or expatriates interested in obtaining a U.S. accredited degree.

In addition, some of these institutions, such as Broward Community College in Ecuador, provide students with a possible gateway to a degree program in the United States. As is often the role of community colleges within the United States, students may study for their first two years at a campus such as Broward and then transfer to a four-year institution.

TABLE 6.2: U.S.-BASED UNIVERSITIES WITH LATIN AMERICAN BRANCH CAMPUSES

Campus Name	Importing Nation	Exporting Nation	Website
Alliant International University Mexico City Campus	Mexico	United States	www.alliantmexico.com
Ave Maria University Latin American Campus	Nicaragua	United States	http://amulac.avemaria.edu
Broward College Ecuador	Ecuador	United States	www.browardecuador.com
Endicott College Mexico	Mexico	United States	www.endicott.edu/Mexico.aspx
Florida State University Panama	Panama	United States	http://panama.fsu.edu

Foreign-Owned Campuses

Foreign-owned campuses are owned by foreign educational providers and afford students the opportunity to earn an academic degree in a Latin American country. Unlike IBCs, foreign-owned campuses do not offer a degree in the name of the foreign owner, and the degree is likely to have only local accreditation, not accreditation from the United States. This type of arrangement, where the local campus name is different from that of the foreign owner, can often make it difficult to determine ownership. For example, when Manipal University in India purchased the American University of Antigua (AUA) in the Caribbean in 2008, it chose to allow AUA to continue to operate in its own name and retain its curriculum (Kinser & Lane, 2012). However, this ownership arrangement is not readily transparent to outside observers, particularly when the foreign education provider obtains ownership of an existing campus, which has been a strategy of many U.S.-based for-profit education providers.

Educational conglomerates such as the Apollo Group (owner of the University of Phoenix), Laureate International Universities, and Whitney International own a myriad of campuses throughout the world, including in Latin America (Kinser & Levy, 2006). Rather than opening branch campuses in their own names, these educationally focused corporations tend to pursue an international expansion strategy that includes purchasing local campuses with existing brand recognition. This allows foreign education providers to take advantage of the local legitimacy already garnered by the campus—legitimacy that would likely have to be rebuilt if the institution's name were to be changed.

Recently, Latin America has become a more attractive market for these types of acquisitions. With the population explosion over the past decade, the number of young people in the region interested in obtaining a college degree has increased significantly. As many public sectors of higher education remain underfunded, this demographic shift has resulted in a substantial expansion in the number of private institutions. With burgeoning enrollments, many of these institutions appear to be lucrative investments for foreign investors, including several large for-profit education companies.

The Latin University of Costa Rica is an excellent example of this sort of outpost. This institution, founded in 1979, evolved into one of the largest private universities in Costa Rica, serving more than 16,000 students in an array of undergraduate and graduate programs accredited by the Costa Rican National Accreditation System for Higher Education. In 2008, it was acquired by Laureate International Universities, which in 2010 merged it with another Laureate-owned campus, the InterAmerican University of Costa Rica. Continuing to operate under the name of the Latin University of Costa Rica, the new institution has enrollments of more than 30,000 students enrolled in two campuses and eight outreach centers across the country. This is just one of 30 Latin American universities that is part of Laureate, a network that includes institutions in Brazil, Chile, Costa Rica, Ecuador, Honduras, Mexico, Panama, and Peru.

Outreach Offices and Study Abroad Centers

Offices or centers that provide an array of opportunities or services for faculty, staff, and students from the home campus are another form of educational outposts. These outposts support activities that originate on the home campus, but are focused on local contacts and engagements in Latin America. An example is the academic center that New York University (NYU) operates in Buenos Aires, Argentina. This center provides students enrolled in academic programs in New York City the opportunity to study abroad in Latin America in order to enhance their Spanish language skills and learn more about Argentine culture.[6]

Examples of more recent innovation are the social laboratories that Columbia University's Graduate School of Architecture, Planning, and Preservation is creating in cities around the world, including Rio de Janeiro, Brazil. The School describes the Studio-X program this way:

The global network of Studio-X spaces that we are building is a new kind of international workshop in which the best minds from Columbia University can think together with the best minds in Latin America, the Middle East, Africa, Eastern Europe, and Asia. Each Studio-X is located in the liveliest part of the historic downtown of a leadership city at the heart of a major region of the world…. Studio-X is not a typical university branch aiming to export leadership education and research around the globe. On the opposite, our colleagues around the world are the leaders in a cross-cultural, cross-disciplinary, and cross-continental exchange within and between diverse regions. Those regions undergoing the most radical transformation have the most to teach us about the future of cities. The continuous flow of exciting ideas and people between these sister Studio-X spaces turns the simple idea of an open collaborative studio into an unprecedented global network aimed at the brightest possible future.[7]

Since many urban planning innovations are occurring outside of New York City, Columbia needed a way to connect directly with the problems and solutions in some of the world's fastest growing cities in order to educate the next generation of architects, engineers, and planners. Creating a social laboratory in the heart of Rio de Janeiro helps to connect students in New York with learning opportunities in Brazil.

Outreach offices are a further example of these types of centers, such as the one operated by the State University of New York (SUNY) in Mexico City.[8] This office, which is owned and operated by SUNY, helps to facilitate existing and future research and academic partnerships between the 64 SUNY campuses in New York and higher education institutions in Mexico. In addition, several SUNY research laboratories have agreements or memorandums of understanding with partner institutes or laboratories in Mexico to study a range of topics from nanotechnology to bioinformatics. This type of outpost helps to build connections in the foreign country, facilitating relationship building, networking, and partnering.

Expansion of CBHE

As previously noted, the literature on Latin American higher education has mostly focused on the tensions between public and private sectors. However, a new dichotomy now exists: domestic versus foreign providers. While a handful of studies have examined the internationalization of higher education activities in Latin America (e.g., de Wit et al., 2005; Gacel-Avila, 2007; Schwartzman, 2010), there have been no studies on the rise of foreign education providers in the region, even though foreign education providers have become actors in Latin America's higher education sector.

I would like to briefly compare the reasons that underlie the growth of CBHE with the typology of private higher education expansion first developed by Levy

(1986) in his study of Latin America. Levy found that private higher education institutions developed because of one of three reasons: (1) to provide something better than what is available in the public sector; (2) to provide something different from what is available in the public sector; or (3) to provide access to those who are not able to attend the private sector. It is worth noting that more than 20 years later, Levy (2008, p. 26) noted that most private higher education institutions continue to "fit pretty clearly (even when not fully) into one category."

In other analyses, it was found that some forms of CBHE "fit [Levy's] categories; however, this group of institutions does not seem to fit clearly into any one category and they 'fit' in ways not usually defined in the academic literature" (Lane, 2011a, p. 374). That is, much like private higher education, CBHE partnerships and outposts developed to meet a variety of different needs. This section provides a preliminary analysis of the extent to which the expansion of CBHE in Latin America aligns with the Levy typology.

The conclusions drawn here are limited in two important ways. First, this is not a systematic examination of CBHE, nor are the partnerships or outposts selected in a scientific sample. While these conclusions are made in the aggregate, the cultural, political, and regulatory environments of each country vary and will likely have differential effects on the development of CBHE within their borders. Second, data about this form of higher education in Latin America are extremely limited. As a result, the chapter relies on a combination of scholarly literature, media coverage, and institutional reports. Despite these limitations, this chapter provides an overview of the diversity of CBHE, with the hope that future work will be able examine the phenomenon in more depth and within particular country contexts.

Something Superior

Many of the partnerships appear to fit into the category of providing something superior to that available in the home country. The partnerships sought by Latin American governments and institutions target countries with well-respected higher education systems (e.g., Germany, the United Kingdom, the United States). The language of many agreements suggests a desire to partner with institutions that have well-regarded reputations.

Something Different

Another driving force of the development of CBHE is the desire to provide something different from what is available from domestic providers. The development of international branch campuses is usually motivated by a need to provide a style of education different from what is available locally. In this case, a handful of U.S.-based institutions have developed branches to provide Latin American students with access to a U.S. education without having to travel to the United States. In addition, some of the partnerships target particular types of education (e.g., STEM programs), with the goal of providing Latin American students with high-quality training in areas that may not be readily available in the home county.

Something More

Growing populations and growing interest in higher education also seem to be drivers of CBHE. Much as unmet demand for higher education led to the development of many private higher education providers, so too has the most recent unmet demand for higher education fostered a growing interest by many foreign education providers. Most notable are the for-profit higher education conglomerates that are purchasing private higher education institutions throughout Latin America.

Economic Competitiveness

Economic competitiveness is a driving force that is not captured by the Levy typology (Lane, 2012). Governments in Latin America are looking for ways to create a more globally competitive workforce, foster domestic research and innovation, and improve their overall economic productivity. To do so, some governments have decided to look for assistance from nations with well-developed higher education institutions. Brazil and Chile have partnered with institutions in the United States in the hope that what is learned from these institutions will help build their innovation infrastructure and economic productivity. In her 2008 visit to California, Chilean president Michelle Bachelet noted that Chilean students who attended UC-Davis in the 1960s to study agronomy led the development of Chiles's agricultural export industry.

Conclusion

Higher education in Latin America is transforming through the growing number of CBHE activities. This chapter summarizes the types of partnerships and foreign education outposts in Latin America that involve U.S.-based colleges and universities. More than partnerships, U.S.-based institutions also own several types of foreign educational outposts, such as international branch campuses, foreign-owned institutions, and outreach and study abroad centers. These outposts serve as physical extensions of the U.S. institutions and provide educational opportunities for both local and foreign students. The reasons for the development of CBHE are diverse and seem to be driven by a combination of needing to provide something better, something different, and simply more access. There also is an underlying desire among governments to use CBHE to help improve their nation's economic competitiveness. More research is needed on this topic, as CBHE is an increasingly important aspect in the development of higher education in Latin America.

NOTES

[1] Memorandum of Understanding between National Science Foundation, United States of America, and the Federal Agency for the Support and Evaluation of Graduate Education of the Federative Republic of Brazil on Dimensions of Biodiversity, signed 2011: http://www.state.gov/p/wha/rls/2011/158683.htm

[2] U.S. Department of State Fact Sheet on United States-Chile Cooperation on Education: http://www.state.gov/p/wha/rls/fs/2011/158622.htm

[3] The Brazil Scientific Mobility Program: http://www.iie.org/Programs/Brazil-Scientific-Mobility

[4] There are also joint-degree programs in which there is a shared curriculum between two institutions and the student receives a joint degree, but Gacel-Avila (2009) found that the administrative complexity of such programs makes them unusual in their international setting.

[5] While there has been a rise in the number of institutions providing students with educational opportunities through distance learning, such activities are not included in an FEP, since they usually do not entail the institution maintaining a physical presence in the foreign country.

[6] NYU Buenos Aires http://www.nyu.edu/global/global-academic-centers1/buenos-aires.html

[7] About Studio-X: http://www.arch.columbia.edu/studiox/about

[8] SUNY Mexico Overview: http://www.suny.edu/InternationalPrograms/mex1.cfm

REFERENCES

Arocena, R., & Sutz, J. (2005). Latin American universities: From an original revolution to an uncertain transition. *Higher Education*, 50, 573–592.

Balán, J., & García de Fanelli, A. M. (1997). El sector privado de la educación superior: Políticas públicas y sus resultados recientes en cinco países de América Latina. In R. Kent (Ed.), *Los temas críticos de la educación superior en América Latina, Vol. 2.* (pp. 9–93). Mexico City, Mexico: Fondo de Cultura Económica-CEDES.

Boas, T. (2008, July 12). *Chile-California: A partnership for the twenty-first century.* Retrieved from http://www.clas.berkeley.edu/events/spring2008/06-12-08-bachelet/BacheletBoasArticle.pdf

C-BERT. (2012). *List of international branch campuses.* Retrieved from Global Higher Education website: http://www.globalhighered.org/branchcampuses.php

de Wit, H., Jaramillo, I. C., Gacel-Avila, J., & Knight, J. (Eds.). (2005). *Higher education in Latin America: The international dimension.* Washington, DC: World Bank.

Gacel-Avila, J. (2007). The process of internationalization of Latin American higher education. *Journal of Studies in International Education, 11*(3), 400–409.

Gacel-Avila, J. (2009). *Joint and double degree programmes in Latin America: Patterns and trends.* London, UK: Observatory on Borderless Higher Education.

Kinser, K., & Lane, J. E. (2012). The multinational university: Moving beyond the international branch campus. *International Higher Education, 66,* 2–3.

Kinser, K., & Levy, D. L. (2006). For-profit higher education: U.S. tendencies, international echoes. *International Handbook of Higher Education, 18*(1), 107–119.

Lane, J. E. (2011a). Importing private higher education: International branch campuses. *Journal of Comparative Policy Analysis, 13*(4), 367–381.

Lane, J. E. (2011b). Global expansion of international branch campuses: Managerial and leadership challenges. In J. E. Lane, & K. Kinser (Eds.), *Multi-national colleges & universities: Leadership, administration, and governance of international branch campuses (New directions for higher education)*. San Francisco, CA: Jossey-Bass.

Lane, J. E. (2012). Higher education and economic competitiveness. In J. E. Lane & D. B. Johnstone (Eds.), *Colleges and universities as economic drivers: Measuring and building success* (pp. 1–27). Albany, NY: SUNY Press.

Lane, J. E., & Kinser, K. (2011a). Reconsidering privatization in cross-border engagements: The sometimes public nature of private activity. *Higher Education Policy, 24*, 255–273.

Lane, J. E., & Kinser, K. (Eds.). (2011b). *Multi-national colleges & universities: Leadership, administration, and governance of international branch campuses.* San Francisco, CA: Jossey-Bass.

Lane, J. E., & Owens, T. (2012). The international dimensions of economic development. In J. E. Lane & D. B. Johnstone (Eds.), *Colleges and universities as economic drivers: Measuring and building success.* Albany, NY: SUNY Press.

Lawton, W., & Katsomitros, A. (2012). *International branch campuses: Data and developments.* London, UK: Observatory on Borderless Higher Education.

Levy, D. C. (1986). *Higher education and the state in Latin America: Private challenges to public dominance.* Chicago, IL: The University of Chicago Press.

McBurnie, G., & Ziguras, C. (2007). *Transnational education: Issues and trends in offshore higher education.* London, UK: Routledge.

Naidoo, V. (2010). Transnational higher education: Why it happens and who benefits? *International Higher Education, 58,* 6–7.

Obst, D., Kuder, M., & Banks, C. (2011). *Joint and double degree programs in the global context: Report on an international survey.* New York, NY: Institute of International Education.

Sanders, D. (2012, April 5). *HCC and Brazil announce partnership to build workforce.* Retrieved from http://sites.hccs.edu/mediaroom/2012/04/hcc-and-brazil-announce-partnership-to-build-workforce/

Schwartzman, S. (2010, April 10). *Changing universities and academic outreach* (Paper prepared for the New Century Scholar's program, Fulbright Commission). Retrieved from http://www.schwartzman.org.br/sitesimon/?p=1573&lang=en-us

Staley, O., & Goldman, H. (2011, December 19). Cornell, Technion are chosen by New York City to create an engineering campus. *Bloomberg.* Retrieved from http://www.businessweek.com/news/2011-12-20/cornell-and-technion-chosen-by-nyc-for-engineering-campus.html

Theiler, J.C. (2005). Internationalization of higher education in Argentina. In H. de Wit, I. C. Jaramillo, J. Gacel-Avila, & J. Knight (Eds.), *Higher education in Latin America: The international dimension* (pp. 71–110). Washington, DC: World Bank.

USAID. (1997). *New partnership initiative (NPI) resource guide: A strategic guide to development partnering.* Report of the NPI Learning Team. Washington, DC: United States Agency for International Development.

Chapter Seven

TOWARD 100,000 STRONG: WESTERN HEMISPHERE ACADEMIC EXCHANGES

MEGHANN CURTIS, DEPUTY ASSISTANT SECRETARY OF STATE FOR
ACADEMIC PROGRAMS, U.S. DEPARTMENT OF STATE

LISA KRAUS, POLICY ADVISER, BUREAU OF EDUCATIONAL AND
CULTURAL AFFAIRS, U.S. DEPARTMENT OF STATE

Peace, prosperity, and democracy throughout the Western Hemisphere are central concerns to U.S. national security. With 50 million people of Hispanic or Latino heritage living in the United States ("The Hispanic Population," 2011), relations with Latin America are a foreign policy priority and of critical domestic importance as well. Only by working together as partners can all the nations of this hemisphere meet the common challenge of creating a future in which our societies can thrive together. And through what Secretary of State Hillary Rodham Clinton calls "the power of proximity" (Clinton, 2012), the United States can help lead the region in pursuit of these goals.

Strong partnerships in the region are critical to both U.S. domestic and global strategic interests. The countries of the Western Hemisphere are the destination of approximately 42 percent of U.S. exports. Science and technology innovations have accelerated through cooperative partnerships and are key to shared sustainable growth. Working collaboratively across borders in the region is necessary to attain energy security and to combat transnational crime and narcotrafficking. Our partners in the Americas are also key allies through multilateral organizations in the global effort to promote democracy, rule of law, social inclusion, and human rights around the world.

Building on cooperative initiatives in the region, U.S. participation in the 2012 Summit of the Americas highlighted practical ways that countries and societies in the Americas are coming together to solve problems and build a more successful and interconnected future. At the Summit, President Barack Obama reinforced the spirit of partnership, announcing initiatives to expand regional broadband capacity, innovative efforts for social inclusion and development, collaboration to improve citizen security, and support for Colombia's Connect 2022 initiative to expand electrical connectivity throughout the Americas.

At the center of these partnerships—and U.S. strategy in the region—are educational exchanges, which help us establish a strong foundation for empowering the best innovators, entrepreneurs, and leaders of today to meet all these challenges.

100,000 Strong in the Americas

At the 2012 Summit President Obama reaffirmed support for 100,000 Strong in the Americas and underscored the centrality of education to our broader efforts. Announced by the President in Santiago, Chile, in March 2011, 100,000 Strong in the Americas aims to increase the flow of students between Latin America and the Caribbean and the United States to 100,000 in each direction. At its core, this initiative is about creating opportunities, both at the household and the national level. With 100,000 Strong, the U.S. government seeks to equip students of the United States and Latin America with new experiences to build the knowledge, skills, and self-reliance they need to increase income and expand opportunities for employment in a globally competitive world. At the same time, educational exchanges are integral to sustaining academic excellence in our higher education institutions. 100,000 Strong offers valuable opportunities for colleges and universities across the United States and Latin America and the Caribbean to expand their footprint and reputation overseas. It is also diversifying U.S. campuses, and not simply with economically privileged students who have the means to study abroad. Through 100,000 Strong, we are prioritizing our efforts to expand academic opportunities for students from disadvantaged backgrounds, historically underserved populations, and students with disabilities.

Getting to 100,000: Diplomacy and Programs

Getting to 100,000 exchanges in each direction will be no small task. According to *Open Doors*, an annual report on student mobility published by the Institute of International Education with financial support from the U.S. Department of State, 64,021 students from Latin America and the Caribbean studied in the United States in the 2011–2012 academic year and 39,871 students from the United States studied abroad in Latin America and the Caribbean in the 2010–2011 academic year (Chow & Bhandari, in press).[1]

The U.S. government is working with foreign governments, universities and colleges, and the private sector to reach the 100,000 Strong goal. Throughout the hemisphere, U.S. embassies and consulates, Fulbright commissions, Binational Centers,[2] and EducationUSA advising centers are joining host governments, schools, universities, businesses, and nongovernmental organizations (NGOs) to advise students on the steps toward international study and the wealth of host institution options, to prepare them with appropriate language training, and to provide scholarships that ultimately make these exchanges possible. Overall, we are pursuing four lines of effort to achieve our goal: advising students and governments, engaging key countries through strategic dialogues, offering both merit-based and need-based scholarships, and increasing relevant language instruction.

Advising Students and Governments

The U.S. higher education system, with more than 4,000 accredited colleges and universities, is complex and decentralized. Today, the United States is home to 2,774 four-year higher education institutions and 1,721 community colleges. Although the diversity of the U.S. system is central to its worldwide preeminence, this complexity and decentralized nature also renders the system challenging to prospective international students. To overcome this hurdle, the U.S. government introduces students to the U.S. system by providing virtual and in-person advising services. It also convenes stakeholders from governments and institutions of higher education across borders and participates in formal bilateral consultations, or "strategic dialogues," with partner governments to expand higher education exchange.

The U.S. government's central vehicle for educational advising is the EducationUSA advising network. With 109 advising centers throughout Latin America, EducationUSA is critical to reaching 100,000 Strong goals. EducationUSA (http://educationusa.state.gov) is a network of U.S.-government-supported advising centers that connects U.S. higher education institutions with international students. Across Latin America and the Caribbean, EducationUSA advising centers provide accurate, comprehensive, and current information about opportunities for study in the United States. Three highly experienced regional educational advising coordinators provide training, guidance, and support to the network throughout Latin

America. For students who are admitted into U.S. institutions, the advising centers conduct predeparture orientations to help prepare them to take full advantage of academic and cultural life on U.S. campuses.

Opportunity Funds from the Bureau of Educational and Cultural Affairs are available through EducationUSA advising centers in 14 countries in the region. This mechanism supports highly talented students from economically disadvantaged backgrounds in Latin America with funds to defray the up-front costs of applying to U.S. institutions. More than 400 students from Latin America have benefited from this program since 2006. EducationUSA advisers also serve as resources for U.S. higher education institutions, helping them to understand local educational systems and the best ways to reach students who may be interested in U.S. study. Advisers may also guide U.S. institutions in identifying high-quality local partner institutions to host American students in Latin America.

In June 2012, the Department of State brought together more than 450 U.S. higher education professionals at the third annual EducationUSA Forum in Washington, DC, to raise awareness of the resources our worldwide educational advising network offers and to discuss strategies for attracting foreign students to U.S. colleges and universities. The event highlighted exchange opportunities with Latin America and new Latin American government scholarship programs. EducationUSA regional educational advising coordinators and advisers from nine countries presented the latest trends in student mobility in Latin America.

In tandem with EducationUSA's grass-roots work, bilateral strategic dialogues— which have been a hallmark of the Obama administration's foreign policy approach—have provided a valuable forum to engage foreign governments on educational exchange issues. Strategic dialogues enhance bilateral cooperation on everything from trade to security to climate change by providing forums for setting long-term goals through regular high-level meetings. On the education front, the dialogues provide a mechanism for expanding collaboration between higher education sectors, leading to increased student mobility between the United States and other countries. Annual meetings with Brazil and Colombia have had positive results in increasing student mobility.

Of the many examples of hemispheric progress on education exchange, perhaps none is as considerable as the U.S.–Brazilian connection. President Obama and Brazilian President Dilma Rousseff share a commitment to an innovative U.S.–Brazil education partnership that addresses the needs of a twenty-first-century workforce. Both presidents believe the prosperity of their countries is intrinsically linked to the education of their people. The U.S.–Brazil Global Partnership Dialogue, first convened in March 2010, and the resulting agreement on education, outlines a strategy to realize the two leaders' goals to expand academic and research exchanges between our two countries. To achieve these objectives, President Rousseff and the government of Brazil launched the Brazil Scientific Mobility Program, known in Portuguese as Ciência Sem Fronteiras, to send Brazilian students abroad over the next four years to study and conduct research in STEM fields (science, technology, engineering, and mathematics). The Brazilian government will fund 75,000 Brazilian students through the program, and the private sector will support an additional 26,000 scholarships. The Brazilian government expects half of the students to study in the United States, giving this program the potential to make a major contribution toward reaching the 100,000 Strong in the Americas goal.

Through collaboration with the Brazilian Federal Agency for Support and Evaluation of Graduate Education (CAPES) and the National Council for Scientific and Technological Development (CNPq), the U.S. Government strives to connect the two countries' higher education communities and create university networks; encourage the placement of Brazilian students at U.S. universities, colleges, and community colleges; support a broad spectrum of short- and longer-term academic and research opportunities at all levels; and promote the overall expansion of U.S. student and research exchanges to Brazil. U.S. efforts are helping our Brazilian partners navigate the American higher education system and connect with the community. Since the program's launch, the 24 EducationUSA advising centers in Brazil have conducted extensive outreach to inform prospective students and faculty of U.S. program requirements and the application process and provide predeparture orientation sessions to students. In January 2012, U.S. colleges and universities welcomed the first group of 650 undergraduate students. By the end of 2012, 2,500 Brazilian students will have arrived at U.S. colleges and universities, with more students anticipated to arrive for the spring semester in 2013.

The U.S. government is also implementing an English language strategy in Brazil that is at the forefront of public diplomacy. This strategy responds to both the Brazil Scientific Mobility Program and to the Brazilian government's recognition that greater English proficiency will bolster its international standing, meet its social and economic inclusion goals, and prepare its workforce to host the upcoming World Cup and Olympic Games. The U.S. government has ramped up English language initiatives in Brazil, increasing the number of English Language Fellows and English Language Specialists to reach a wider demographic, perhaps best represented by a new strong partnership with the government of Pernambuco (Recife) state. Brazil's 38 Binational Centers (BNCs) implement these projects as well as a new intensive English language immersion program, English[3] ("English-cubed"), to prepare university students for success on U.S. campuses. The U.S. government is pursuing options for bringing the best of America's education technology to assist the Brazilian government in its distance education and workforce training goals. Student achievement in English builds from teaching excellence, so the U.S. government is also working closely with CAPES for professional development of English teachers including more than 500 Brazilian public school English teachers who will arrive in January 2013 for an exchange program.

The dialogue between the United States and Brazil has also led to the expansion of the Fulbright Foreign Language Teaching Assistant Program in partnership with the government of Brazil to promote the study of Portuguese language and culture in the United States and to encourage American students to study in Brazil. Of the approximately 236 million Portuguese speakers worldwide, the 2009 U.S. Census reports that 731,282 people speak Portuguese or Portuguese Creole at home in the United States (U.S. Census Bureau, 2012). Brazilian educators serve as native Portuguese language resources in the classroom and in cultural activities as they pursue their own nondegree studies in pedagogy, curriculum development, and English language at accredited postsecondary U.S. educational institutions. Also in March 2012, the two governments announced the expansion of teaching and research exchange opportunities in science and technology through the new Fulbright–Science Without Borders Scholar and Distinguished Chair Awards for midcareer researchers and senior faculty in the United States. U.S. scholars will be affiliated with top Brazilian universities and research centers in their areas of specialization, fostering increased cooperation and institutional collaboration between applied researchers in science, technology, and innovation fields. As part of a joint effort to expand Fulbright exchange opportunities in a variety of academic disciplines, the governments of the United States and Brazil are doubling the number of Fulbright Scholar Awards for Brazilians and introducing a new Fulbright Post-Doctoral Award for U.S. and Brazilian researchers.

The U.S. government is also collaborating with partners in the private sector to promote and expand academic exchange opportunities between U.S. Historically Black Colleges and Universities (HBCUs) and Brazilian universities. These efforts are in support of the U.S.–Brazil Joint Action Plan to Eliminate Racial and Ethnic Discrimination and Promote Equality (Joint Action Plan). The Joint Action Plan began in 2008 as a government-to-government agreement, and expanded to include participation of civil society, academia, and the private sector. It promotes increased access to education, economic opportunities and labor, the justice system, health, and environmental justice for African descendant, indigenous, and other marginalized communities in both countries. In 2011, an alliance of HBCUs and CAPES signed a memorandum of understanding (MOU) under the education aspect of the Joint Action Plan. This MOU has already increased the diversity of U.S. institutions that receive Brazilian students and opens the door to additional exchange on STEM, student recruitment, retention, and other issues.

Alongside the tremendous advances in the U.S.–Brazilian education partnership are more modest but equally promising developments in a U.S.–Colombia education partnership. The first meeting of the U.S.–Colombia High Level Partnership Dialogue (HLPD) took place in Bogota in October 2010. At this time, the United States and Colombia signed an Action Plan on Racial Equality to facilitate access to education for marginalized Afro-Colombian and indigenous students through English teaching, leadership, and academic exchanges. In July 2011, under the HLPD, a new culture and education working group outlined plans to enhance collaboration between the United States and Colombia on programs and policies to improve English proficiency, increase student mobility between Colombia and the United States, and provide information on U.S. community college study opportunities. In July 2012, the United States participated in a third HLPD delegation and announced plans to double professional development programs for teachers and to multiply the impact of the Fulbright Program and deliver on the 2010 Action Plan through Fulbright Alumni Social Inclusion Impact Grants, which will allow alumni from underserved sectors of Colombian society to undertake community service projects that promote education and volunteerism. In support of English language learning, a new 3-D English language learning video game, Trace Effects, will be launched at Binational Centers and public libraries around the country.

Expanding Scholarship Opportunities: Fulbright and Beyond
Predating the launch of 100,000 Strong and the recent cumulative swell in hemispheric education cooperation are the 60-year running Fulbright Program and other State Department–funded academic exchange programs. These programs, which are based on transparent, merit-based selection processes, promote diverse participation and inclusion and emphasize academic achievement and leadership development. The collective energy of academic program participants—and by extension, the energy of their peers, their home and host institutions, and their communities—strengthen people-to-people ties in the region and help the United States meet a variety of policy goals including 100,000 Strong.

Since its inauguration in 1946, the Fulbright Program has played an integral role in U.S. foreign relations by providing more than 310,000 participants worldwide with the opportunity to study, teach and conduct research, and exchange ideas. Whether the challenge is transforming conflict into dialogue, conducting research on pandemic issues such as HIV/AIDS, designing an efficient energy grid, or even creating artwork that reflects and draws on cross-cultural experiences, Fulbrighters have been at the front lines of international education and cooperation for more than 60 years. Today, Fulbright is recognized as one of the world's foremost educational exchange programs, and it is at the centerpiece of the U.S. commitment to engage the countries of Latin America to expand educational opportunities.

The State Department's Bureau of Educational and Cultural Affairs (ECA) administers the Fulbright Program under policy guidelines established by the J. William Fulbright Foreign Scholarship Board with the assistance of binational commissions and foundations in 50 countries, U.S. embassies in more than 100 other countries, and cooperating agencies in the United States. Within Latin America, binational Fulbright commissions operate in Argentina, Brazil, Chile, Colombia, Ecuador,

Mexico, Peru, and Uruguay. In 2011, governments in the region provided $25 million to support the Fulbright Program, and the private sector contributed an additional $6.5 million. These public and private sector investments, which have nearly tripled since 2000, demonstrate the shared commitment to education in the region.

Since the inception of the Fulbright Program in the Western Hemisphere, more than 37,500 grants have been awarded, including about 1,400 grants for new and continuing students in 2011 (Table 7.1). The core Fulbright Program includes four major programs for U.S. students, U.S. scholars, visiting (foreign) students, and visiting scholars. Within these categories, additional program components, such as the Fulbright Faculty Development Program, have brought thousands of Latin American students, scholars, teachers, and faculty to the United States for graduate study and related research.

The Hubert H. Humphrey Fellowship Program, which is also a Fulbright activity, brings early and midcareer professionals from countries that are in development and transition to the United States for a year of nondegree, graduate-level study and professional development. In the 33 years the Humphrey Program has been in place, 836 emerging Latin American leaders have studied in the United States, including Ellen Northfleet, who was appointed Brazil's first female Supreme Court Justice in 2000.

TABLE 7.1: FISCAL YEAR 2011 FULBRIGHT PROGRAM PARTICIPANTS

Program	U.S. Participants	Latin American Participants
Fulbright Scholars (including Fulbright Specialists)	180	114
Fulbright Students (including Fulbright Faculty Development, Fulbright Foreign Language Teaching Assistant, and Fulbright English Teaching Assistant Programs)	288	1,060
Hubert H. Humphrey Fellowship Program		38

Sustaining interaction with and among the alumni of its exchanges is a priority for ECA. Worldwide, 28 Fulbright alumni have served as heads of state or government, 11 Fulbright alumni have been elected to the United States Congress, 78 have received Pulitzer Prizes, and 44 alumni from 12 countries have received Nobel Prizes. Current President of Chile Sebastián Piñera, President of Colombia Juan Manuel Santos, and Governor General of Belize Colville Norbert Young are all alumni of the Fulbright Program (participating in 1973, 1980, and 1991, respectively).

The Fulbright Program has a long and distinguished tradition that has earned academic respect. It is also flexible, innovative, and responsive to U.S. foreign policy priorities. Recent Fulbright initiatives have tailored the program to address public policy capacity development needs and to bring science and technology researchers together across borders. To strengthen the public sector in developing countries, the new Fulbright Public Policy Fellowship Program allows U.S. citizens to serve in professional placements within foreign government ministries or institutions in selected countries worldwide. This program provides an opportunity for U.S. participants to work side by side with government representatives of other countries to tackle the toughest public policy problems of the day. The first cohort of fellows bound for Latin America and the Caribbean arrived in fall 2012 in the Dominican Republic, Guatemala, Haiti, and Jamaica. The seven government placements for the fellows in the region included Ministries of Commerce, Education, Energy and Mines, Public Health and Population, Planning, Youth, and the Office of the Prime Minister. In these positions, fellows will advance public policy research agendas, foster mutual understanding, and build ties between the United States and partner countries.

Launched in 2010, the Fulbright Regional Network for Applied Research (Fulbright NEXUS) Program supports long-term U.S. goals and foreign government priorities by fostering innovative and multidisciplinary research to fight poverty and inequality while bolstering science and technology networks throughout the Americas. The Fulbright NEXUS Program brings together researchers, applied practitioners, members of civil society and the public and private sectors for a year of collaborative research that moves beyond theory and into practice. NEXUS Scholars participate in a series of seminar meetings in two Western Hemisphere countries; a final plenary in Washington, DC; and a research exchange. They cultivate partnerships with local, national, and regional stakeholders, linking science and policy through innovative projects that have long-term regional impact. In 2012, the Fulbright NEXUS Program will give special emphasis to the topic of global climate change and adaptation strategies in the Americas. Previous projects have included the design of a low-wind-speed turbine for household use, a hydropower plant that would bring electricity and economic development to a remote region of Jamaica, and a cost-effective telemedicine kit to improve health care access for rural Colombians who live hours from the nearest medical facility.

One challenge for many talented students from disadvantaged backgrounds is English language proficiency. To address this problem, the Department of State offers many incoming international fellows three to nine months of preacademic intensive English. One excellent example is the Fulbright Equal Opportunity Program in Chile, which supports doctoral study each year for 25 Chilean students from outside Santiago and from lower socioeconomic backgrounds. The program, which is funded primarily by the Chilean government, provides candidates with in-country English language instruction followed by preacademic English coursework in the United States prior to their doctoral programs. The College Horizons Outreach Program is another example of U.S. government support to increase access to higher education for marginalized high school students. This program provides English teaching, academic advising, and mentoring to hundreds of African descendant and indigenous youth in Bolivia, Colombia, Ecuador, Haiti, Nicaragua, Panama, and Peru.

Another effective program for increasing diversity in international education is the Benjamin A. Gilman International Scholarship Program, which awards study abroad scholarships to financially disadvantaged U.S. undergraduate students who receive federally funded Pell Grants and have been traditionally underrepresented in international educational exchanges. The proportion of Gilman Scholars who are African American, Latino, or Asian American is, respectively, nearly four times, nearly triple, or nearly double when compared to the national rate for study abroad. In addition to providing opportunities for disadvantaged students, the Gilman Scholarship also encourages study abroad in nontraditional destinations. A total of 383 Gilman Scholars studied throughout Latin America in academic year 2011–2012 and summer 2012 in 18 countries, with Argentina, Costa Rica, and Brazil being the most popular destinations.

To catalyze younger students' global consciousness, the Department of State also brings students from countries worldwide to the United States for undergraduate study. The Global Undergraduate Exchange Program combines a semester or academic year of undergraduate study with intensive English language instruction, community service, internships, and cultural enrichment (Table 7.2). Study of the U.S. Institutes for Student Leaders are five-week academic programs on U.S. campuses to introduce foreign undergraduates to U.S. society, culture, history, and government. The Community College Initiative (CCI) provides educational and hands-on training opportunities in the fields of business management and administration, tourism and hospitality management, media, information technology, agriculture, and engineering science. It also offers in-depth exposure to U.S. culture and institutions. Currently, students from Brazil, Costa Rica, and Panama participate in the CCI program.

TABLE 7.2: FISCAL YEAR 2011 GLOBAL UNDERGRADUATE EXCHANGE PROGRAM PARTICIPANTS

Program	U.S. Participants	Latin American Participants
Global Undergraduate Program		80
Study of the U.S. Institutes		139
Benjamin A. Gilman Exchange Program	383	
Community College Initiative		57

The Department of State also recognizes the importance of exchanges and professional development for teachers who educate and influence young people around the world. The Teaching Excellence and Achievement (TEA) program and the International Leaders in Education Program (ILEP) together bring approximately 50 to 60 secondary-level teachers each year from Latin America for programs hosted by U.S. graduate schools. The programs include professional development in pedagogical content and methodology, including the use of instructional technology, field experience in a local secondary school, and cultural enrichment. One team of Teaching Excellence and Achievement alumni are working together to expand a peace education project they developed with their U.S. partner teachers. With support from the Department of State Alumni Engagement Innovation Fund (https://alumni.state.gov/aeif) Project Capaz endeavors to establish a culture of peace in secondary schools for 1,200 at-risk youth in Colombia, El Salvador, and Nicaragua.

Promoting Language Study: English, Spanish, and Portuguese
A central part of these exchanges is language instruction. English is widely recognized as the international language of science and business, as well as a key ingredient for helping broaden economic opportunity. Expanding access to English helps talented young people compete for jobs, access higher education and study in the United States, and improve their ability to contribute to the socioeconomic development of their countries.

Throughout Latin America, the Department of State's English Access Microscholarship Program provides scholarships to 4,500 bright, disadvantaged, 13- to 20-year-old students to study English and learn about U.S. culture and democratic principles in their home country. As Access students graduate from the program, new opportunities for employment, continued higher education, and even international exchange programs are within reach. Access alumni also work together to share what they have learned with others. In Guatemala, for example, Access alumni are working in small groups along with their teachers to develop lesson plans and teach English to children and women in their local communities.

The Department of State provides scholarships to young English teachers from the region to come to the United States to refine their teaching skills and increase their English proficiency while helping teach Spanish or Portuguese on U.S. campuses through the Fulbright Foreign Language Teaching Assistant Program. In the other direction, the Fulbright English Teaching Assistant Program, the English Language Fellow Program, and the English Language Specialist Program send Americans overseas to assist with English language instruction, teacher training, and curriculum development. These fellows and specialists are working in Brazil to teach and oversee curriculum implementation in Pernambuco and establish after-school English classes for middle school students from low-income neighborhoods led by volunteer undergraduate English education students. In Paraguay, an English Language Fellow designed weekly inserts for a heavily circulated daily newspaper, along with a teaching guide video demonstrating how to use the inserts for public school teachers to support English teaching. In Ecuador, an English Language Specialist worked with the Ministry of Education to develop in-service English as a foreign language teacher standards and preservice courses at local universities for secondary English teachers. In Venezuela, an English Language Specialist conducted in-service workshops for approximately 200 Venezuelan teachers that focused on pedagogical tools incorporating critical thinking skills into the English language teaching classroom.

Technology holds tremendous potential for increasing the number of English speakers worldwide. ECA's new American English Online portal (http://american english.state.gov) is one way the Department of State is working to increase the circulation of high-quality English language learning resources. Distance learning programs also hold tremendous promise for English language learning. To date, nearly 250 English teaching professionals have participated in ECA's e-Teacher Scholarship Program, which provides online learning opportunities on topics such as critical thinking, assessment, methodology, and differentiated education. In addition, nearly 5,000 English teachers have participated in Shaping the Way We Teach English webinars that provide online, interactive, professional development courses including live sessions with U.S. language experts and the opportunity to exchange best practices through an associated social networking page.

Moving Forward Together

In the twenty-first century, prosperity, security, and democracy for all the people of the Western Hemisphere will depend on building the educational infrastructure to train our innovators, entrepreneurs, and other future leaders. And in a rapidly interconnected world, cross-cultural experiences and the ability to work and thrive across borders will be essential building blocks for success in any country and will strengthen partnerships between countries. By harnessing the transformational power of educational exchange, the Department of State is helping make this goal a reality.

NOTES

[1] Because of data collection methodology and differing academic cycles, the statistics for U.S. student study in other countries lags one year behind the statistics on international student study in the United States in the annual *Open Doors* report.

[2] Binational Centers (BNCs) are private, autonomous, publicly accessible nonprofit institutions dedicated to promoting mutual understanding between the host country and the United States through educational, cultural, and informational programs.

REFERENCES

Chow, P. & Bhandari, R. (In press). *Open doors 2012: Report on international educational exchange.* New York, NY: Institute of International Education.

Clinton, H. R. (2012). *Secretary Clinton's remarks at the White House Conference on Connecting the Americas, April 12, 2012.* Retrieved from http://www.state.gov/secretary/rm/2012/04/187811.htm

The Hispanic Population: 2010. (2011). *2010 Census briefs.* Retrieved from http://www.census.gov/prod/cen2010/briefs/c2010br-04.pdf

U.S. Census Bureau. (2012). *Table 53. Languages spoken at home.* Retrieved from http://www.census.gov/compendia/statab/2012/tables/12s0053.pdf

Chapter Eight

ACADEMIC RESEARCH AND ADVANCED TRAINING: BUILDING UP RESEARCH UNIVERSITIES IN BRAZIL

ELIZABETH BALBACHEVSKY, UNIVERSITY OF SÃO PAULO, BRAZIL

This chapter examines the special conditions that made it possible for Brazil, a late-comer to higher education in Latin America, to build up an impressive and well-established system of public universities marked by their strong orientation toward research and graduate teaching. While all public universities in Brazil share some features that could be taken as preconditions for developing a modern university, not all of them can be classified as real research universities. This analysis used information from the Brazilian Census of Higher Education, carried out by the Ministry of Education, and data collected by the 2007 Brazilian national survey of the academic profession, carried out under the framework of the research network, The Changing Academic Profession (CAP; http://www.uni-kassel.de/wz1/cap/international.ghk).

As acknowledged by the international literature, the most important of these preconditions is the coverage of full-time contracts. The most recent data available for the national census of higher education in Brazil, from 2010, show that 85 percent of all academics employed at public universities in Brazil hold full-time contracts. In the last survey (in 2007) on the Brazilian academic profession, 83 percent of all respondents working in public universities who indicate that they held full-time contract also declared that the contract was their sole professional commitment (INEP, 2011).

Nevertheless, building up research universities is not just a matter of providing good terms of contract for the great majority of the academics or providing good infrastructure. Aside from these more general conditions, research universities are also characterized by the dominance of an academic culture "grounded in individual competence and freedom to choose their own subjects of research, study and reflection" (S. Schwartzman & Balbachevsky, 1997, p. 270). As elaborated in another work (Balbachevsky, 2000), this culture subsumes the role of teaching to the role of research and knowledge production. It is an open culture in which the main source of prestige is the recognition gained from peers in the same field, who are—to a great extent—external to the institution's control (Balbachevsky, 2000, p. 138).

While all public universities in Brazil offer good academic conditions, only a small number of them can be described as real research universities. A major feature of research institutions is their commitment to the graduate education, especially doctoral education: In none of them are fewer than 30 percent of their students enrolled in graduate programs. In some, this proportion reaches 50 percent. Together, these institutions, plus the small but active sector of the federal research institutes, grant more than 85 percent of all doctoral degrees granted in Brazil (CGEE, 2010). This chapter presents some of the most relevant features of these research universities, discusses the special conditions and internal dynamics supporting the emergence of public universities with this profile in Brazil, and explores some challenges posed to the future evolution of these universities.

Research and Regional Universities in Brazil: Distinctive Traits

Diversity is one of the essential characteristics of Brazilian higher education. In 2010 Brazil had more than 2,300 higher education institutions, in both metropolitan areas and small towns around the country. While, by law, all these institutions are supposed to provide similar undergraduate instruction—all of them grant bachelor's degrees—the differences among them are immense. Private institutions represent more than 88 percent of all institutions and 72.5 percent of all enrollments at the undergraduate level.

In the private sector the most usual institutional format is the isolated professional school offering programs in a small number of professional tracks.[1] Nevertheless, the last decade has witnessed a strong process of concentration inside this sector. In 2010, 89 private universities had more than 27.5 percent of all undergraduate enrollments.

The most common institutional format for the public sector is the comprehensive university. The vast majority, 87 percent, of all undergraduate students enrolled in the public sector attend programs offered by universities. Inside the public sector, the most relevant divide is the one created by the graduate education. In late 1960s, when graduate education was first recognized and received support from the federal government,[2] only a few public institutions (both federal and state owned) were well positioned to take advantage of the existing incentives. These institutions created a large number of graduate programs and hired academics with PhDs to staff them. With a great number of PhD holders, these institutions were also able to capture the investments the Brazilian government was mobilizing for science and technology in the 1970s. For the purposes of this chapter, we propose to call these institutions public research universities.

However, in contrast to these public research universities, other public institutions lack the internal conditions for high-level academic work, despite their university status. Inside them, graduate education is a smaller enterprise and tends to be confined to the master's level. Nonetheless, these institutions play a relevant role not only in undergraduate education, but also as a regional source of skills and knowledge. As thus, we propose to call them public regional universities, regardless of whether they are owned by the federal government or some state government.

Public regional universities are marked by a much more diverse internal academic environment than public research universities. Diversity does not come from differences in contracts and conditions of work. These dimensions are more or less homogeneous and derive from the terms of contract accessible to all academic staff. Heterogeneity is produced by contrasts in values, worldviews, and aspirations held by different groups within the academic staff (Balbachevsky, 2000). In fact, inside the Brazilian academic culture there is a strong subculture characterized by the dedication to undergraduate education and by the primacy it attributes to teaching (not implying a commitment to scholarship) over all other activities.

This is a self-referent culture. Inside it, "the professional identity is not defined by the individual's achievements as an independent scholar and researcher but by affiliation to an institution and a group with whom she/he shares the daily problems, achievements, and routines of academic life" (S. Schwartzman & Balbachevsky, 1997, p. 271). For this group, autonomy is to be found in the intrinsic rewards created by the exchange with students inside the classroom. This strategy also implies renouncing the merit-based hierarchy that is one of the foundations of the academic profession. For the academics sharing this worldview, the only acceptable basis for differentiation is that coming from external conditions that could, in theory, be extended to everyone, regardless of considerations about performance, reputation, and so on. This perspective enables us to understand the roots and the centrality of the egalitarian demands inside Brazilian academic culture. It is among this group of academics that "one can find some of the central dilemmas that are common to all process of professionalization: the conflict between the ideals for collectivist trade unions and the individualistic liberal professions; the opposition between the values of personal achievements and those of the professional community; and, consequently, the spaces that are open or closed for intellectual growth, the development of competence, and the strengthening of social responsibilities" (S. Schwartzman & Balbachevsky, 1997, p. 271).

Table 8.1 shows some of the more relevant differences that characterize the quotidian of the academics employed in public research universities and public regional universities in Brazil.

TABLE 8.1: DIFFERENCES IN WORK CONDITIONS IN DIFFERENT SETTINGS IN THE PUBLIC SECTOR IN BRAZIL

	Percentage of academics	
Academics with:	Public research universities	Public regional universities
Full-time contract	91.1%	79.7%
Commitment to more than one academic institution	13.4%	19.9%
Work outside the academic market	13.8%	21.6%
Hold a PhD	94.3%	64.2%
Teaching appointment in graduate education[1]	83.7%	45.3%
Teaching appointment in doctoral programs	47.8%	16.2%

1. Teaching appointment in graduate education includes teaching in academic master's level programs, doctoral programs, or professionally oriented graduate programs.

Source: CAP Survey, Brazil

As one can see, conditions of commitment to academic life differ in research and regional universities. The proportion of academics in research universities with full-time contracts is higher and the proportion of those reporting working responsibilities outside their institution, either with another academic institution and/or outside the academic market, is lower than in regional universities. On the other hand, academics in research universities tend to split their teaching commitments between graduate and undergraduate level, and teaching in doctoral programs is a fairly frequent experience. In regional universities, the majority of the academics are confined to undergraduate level, and only a tiny percentage have experience of teaching (and advising) doctoral candidates.

Another dimension where one can find relevant differences is related to the degree of commitment to research. As it is well acknowledged by the literature, in order to be a full-fledged researcher, besides doing research with some regularity, an academic should be able to bring research findings to the attention of a wider audience, which usually means publishing these findings (Fulton & Trow, 1975), and, following the new trends in internationalization, sustaining regular exchange with peers abroad. In the Brazilian context, researchers should also have the skills and experience to compete for external support for their research activities, since it is not usual for universities, even public ones, to set aside their own resources for research. In the 2007 survey on the Brazilian academic profession, a number of questions were asked that provided information about all these dimensions. When combined, these dimensions allow for the construction of a scale measuring the level of the academic's commitment with the researcher role. This scale is shown in Table 8.2, which ranks the research activity of Brazilian academics from a nonactive role through a fully professionalized researcher with active international connections (i.e., academics reporting success in securing external resources for their research, publishing results, and developing partnerships with colleagues abroad or publishing in collaboration with peers from abroad).

TABLE 8.2: DEGREE OF COMMITMENT WITH RESEARCH ACTIVITY BY TYPE OF INSTITUTION (2007)

	Type of institution	
Degree of commitment with research	Public research universities	Public regional universities
Full researcher with international connections	29.9%	11.8%
Full researcher with only domestic connections	24.4%	15.5%
Doing research and publishing without support	31.0%	44.6%
Doing research without support and without publishing	8.6%	11.1%
Not active as a researcher	6.1%	16.9%
Total (100%)	197	296

Scale's reproducibility index (for public institutions): 0.95

Source: CAP Survey, Brazil

As shown in Table 8.2, the majority of the academics in research universities are full-fledged researchers, doing research, publishing, and counting on external support for their research projects. Inside regional universities, academics with this profile add up to only 27.3 percent, while 28.0 percent are either inactive as researchers or have not published (even if they reported some research in the last three years before the interview, they were not able to refer to any academic product derived from this activity). Whereas 29.9 percent of the academics working in research universities reported some kind of international connection (doing research and/or publishing with peers abroad), this figure drops to only 11.8 percent for those working in regional universities.

Finally, another relevant dimension is the relationship between institutional career and research profile for both kinds of public universities in Brazil. As shown in Table 8.3, for research universities this relationship tends to follow a linear pattern, where academics in higher ranks are also research leaders, with more active and international research profile. Inside regional universities, the pattern runs contrary the expected association.

TABLE 8.3: PATTERNS OF COMMITMENT TO RESEARCH, ACADEMIC RANK, AND INSTITUTIONAL ENVIRONMENT

Type of institution		Academic rank			
		Full professor	Associate professor	Junior	Total
Public research universities	Full-fledged researcher with international connections	56.5%	28.9%	19.2%	29.6%
	Full-fledged researcher with only domestic connections	26.1%	25.6%	21.2%	24.5%
	Partially professionalized researcher	8.7%	40.5%	51.9%	39.8%
	Not active	8.7%	5.0%	7.7%	6.1%
	Total (100%)	23	121	52	196
Public regional universities	Full-fledged researcher with international connections	6.3%	18.2%	4.3%	11.9%
	Full-fledged researcher with only domestic connections	6.3%	22.1%	9.7%	15.6%
	Partially professionalized researcher	45.8%	55.2%	61.3%	55.6%
	Not active	41.7%	4.5%	24.7%	16.9%
	Total (100%)	48	154	93	295

Source: CAP Survey, Brazil

Table 8.3 shows that while only 6.3 percent of the full professors in regional universities display a profile that could be described as mature and internationalized ("full-fledged researcher with international connections"), this percentage is 18.2 percent among the associate professors, and 4.3 percent among the junior staff. So it seems that in regional universities commitment to research tends to be stronger among academics occupying intermediate positions in academic rank.

The explanation for this unusual pattern is that in most public institutions, holding a doctoral degree automatically grants access to the rank of associate professor, but not to full professorship. In the past, for most of the public sector, the lack of academics with the desired qualification induced special rules that bypassed the need of a doctorate for ascending the academic career (for an in-depth analysis of academic careers in Brazilian institutions, see Balbachevsky, 2011). Only the most competitive institutions were able to preserve the requirement of a doctoral degree for candidates ascending to full professorship. Thus, in regional institutions, many members of the older, less qualified generation are now full professors, while the new, better-qualified generation, holding enough academic credentials to compete for research funds, is stuck in the middle of the career rank.

Both the institutional environment and academic degree are relevant for understanding an academic's commitment to research. In each type of institution, academics with doctorates tend to be more involved in research, and most of the academics without doctorates are not active in research. Institutions where almost all faculty members hold doctorate degrees (as in research universities and research institutes) tend to display a more dynamic research environment. But the inner institution's environment creates its own constraints for research. While 58.2 percent of the doctorate holders working in research universities reported success in securing external resources for their research, this proportion drops to 40.4 percent among academics with doctorates working in regional universities.

The Birth of Research Universities in Brazil

Building up universities in Brazil is a quite recent experience. The country's first university law was enacted in 1931, and the first university, The University of Rio de Janeiro (afterward the University of Brazil, later renamed as Federal University of Rio do Janeiro), was founded in the same year. Between the 1930s and 1950s higher education in Brazil experienced its first burst of development. In 1934 the state of São Paulo, the most dynamic regional economy in the country, created its own university, the Universidade de São Paulo. In 1940 the first Catholic university, the Pontifícia University Catholic of Rio de Janeiro, was established, and in the subsequent years other Catholic universities were founded in major cities and state capitals. After 1945, an actual network of federal universities was established, following the principle that each state should have at least one federal university.

In 1968 the federal government, then under military rule, enacted a bill proposing to reform university life. It replaced the old chair system with the department model; introduced the credit system for undergraduate studies; adopted full-time contracts for academics; split the old faculties of science, philosophy, and humanities, allowing for specialized institutes to be created and recognized; and regulated the then incipient graduate education.

Even though these reforms faced some resistance from the old, prestigious professional schools and mistrust from some academics and students, major changes were implemented inside the public sector (for an overview of the 1968 reforms, see Klein, 1992; Durhan, 1998). Between 1972 and 1986, spending by universities in the federal budget grew by a factor of 5.4. Most of this extra money was consumed by implementing full-time contracts for faculty and building up new campuses in the American style in the outskirts of the cities for the federal universities (J. Schwartzman, 1993; Velloso, 1987).

The 1960s reforms were implemented amid an explosive increase in the demand for higher education. In 1960 the total enrollment in higher education was 93,000 students. In 1970 it had jumped to 425,400, and by 1975 it was 1.1 million. Nevertheless, contrary to the experience of other countries in Latin America, the federal government opted to divert access to the private sector, preserving the public universities from the most deleterious effects of massification. In the public sector, entrance examinations were (and still are) used to control the growth of enrollments and limit pressures on the academics' teaching loads.

The almost universal access of faculty to full-time contracts inside public universities and the effects of diverting increased enrollment to the private sector were the first steps toward building up real research-oriented universities inside Brazil. The other steps were the institutionalization of graduate education, the adoption of a consistent set of policies aiming at assuring both growth and quality at this level of education, and the articulation of mechanisms for assuring resources to support academics' steady commitment to research.

The Graduate Foundations of Research

The origins of graduate studies in Brazil can be traced to early experiences with the chair model in 1930s. At that time some universities in Brazil attracted a number of foreign scholars; some of them came in special missions organized by the Brazilian government, and others arrived as refugees from the European crisis of the 1930s. In these earlier experiences, graduate studies were conceived as kind of apprenticeship. Training was mostly informal and gravitated around the assistant's academic responsibilities and dissertation. These earlier experiences in graduate education had little impact on higher education as a whole. It was a small enterprise only organized in some chairs in a small number of universities. The graduate degrees had no currency outside of the academy. In most cases, they were one pathway among others to an academic career.

Graduate education was legally recognized and regulated only in 1965. Its main organizational features were sketched by Report 977, enacted by the Federal Council of Education (known in Brazil as *Parecer Sucupira*). This report created a two-level format for graduate studies, where students were supposed to successfully conclude a master's degree program prior to being accepted into a doctorate program. The regulation of graduate studies is indicative of the government's awareness of the role of this level of education as a domestic alternative to qualify academics for the growing federal network of universities.

The Quest for Evaluation of Graduate Education

Report 977 also conferred on the Ministry of Education's Federal Council of Education (*Conselho Federal de Educação*) the responsibility for graduate programs' accreditation and evaluation. However, early attempts to fulfill this role failed, for the lack of appropriate mechanisms and procedures.

Despite the failure of the first attempts, there were at least two stakeholders interested in developing good standards for the evaluation of graduate programs. For the S&T agencies, the absence of general standards meant that they had few clues in choosing to support or dismiss applications for long-term support for research teams. For the research groups linked to the programs, being recognized as having high quality meant independence from the agencies' internal struggles. Evaluation was also perceived as a key alternative for preserving the legitimacy and prestige of graduate education. The solution was reached when CAPES (Brazilian Federal Agency for Support and Evaluation of Graduate Education, originally in charge of providing scholarships for faculty and graduate students) organized the first general evaluation of graduate programs in 1976. The procedure was supposed to serve as a guideline for allocating the students' scholarships (Castro & Soares, 1986) For this evaluation, CAPES proposed to focus on the collective academic outputs of the researchers formally linked as advisors of each program. In order to ensure credibility for the entire process, the agency enlisted the help of prestigious scholars, who were brought in as consultants to work in committees, one for each discipline. The first round of evaluation was successfully carried out in the same year, and its results were accepted by both the agencies and the community of scholars linked to graduate education.

Eventually, the CAPES evaluation was accepted by all stakeholders as a reference of quality for graduate programs. It successfully connected performance with reward: the better the program evaluation, the greater its chances for accrued support as expressed in students scholarships and research infrastructure and funds. Most important, CAPES evaluation provided an important threshold of quality performance precluding graduate education and, mostly, doctoral programs to spread inside all public universities. As such, it inadvertently produced the concentration of support and competencies necessary for establishing some ambitious research programs that were linked to the best graduate programs and reinforced the visibility and institution wide effects of this level of education inside the few public (and some Catholic) universities where graduate education became fully institutionalized, mobilizing a significant institutional commitment (Balbachevsky & Schwartzman, 2010).

So, one could say that one of the factors explaining the success of Brazilian higher education in building up a strong research profile is hidden in its success in building a strong tier of graduate education, and at the same time, the strong forces sustaining concentration of this endeavor in just a small number of public universities. Graduate education in Brazil emerged in the 1970s as a by-product of the consensus built among political leaders, policymakers, and domestic science leaders around a project that positions science as a core policy for promoting the country's economic development and independence. As it grew, it created the necessary conditions for research to become institutionalized inside a small number of Brazilian universities that had succeeded in developing a robust tier of graduate education. Pivotal to this process was the institutionalization of the procedures related with programs' evaluation. The strong legitimacy of these procedures rested in the work done by the committees of peers that CAPES was able to mobilize for these evaluations. The work of these evaluation committees can be regarded as one the most effective instruments for expediting the institutionalization of all fields of knowledge an in building the foundations of the Brazilian scientific community (S. Schwartzman, 1991).

While the first committees were chosen in an ad hoc procedure among the most influential scientific leaders in Brazil; as the CAPES evaluation became institutionalized, the composition of these committees became more stable, but at the same time, the nomination process converted into an arena where different research traditions and groups struggled to be represented. This process presents few difficulties in areas where scientific consensus is broad, and the research agenda is more or less consensual. But in fields where these characteristics are not present, this struggle was fierce and the committees' decisions had major impacts over the odds of different research traditions (Coutinho, 1996). As quality tends to be defined in terms of what is done by the most powerful groups inside each field, the whole process is, by its nature, very conservative and poses relevant obstacles for the growth of new research areas, especially when they are created in between the rigid boundaries CAPES evaluation defines for different fields.

Building Up Funding Mechanisms for Research

Another decisive step into building up research oriented universities was taken when graduate programs came to be defined as a privileged focus for policies adopted for science and technology (S. Schwartzman, 1991) in the early 1970s. In those years Brazilian S&T policies experienced a major change: For the first time, the Brazilian government attempted to position science and technology as a tool for support economic development. This initiative is best understood if one takes into account the consensus then built between influential scientists (some of them with well-known leftist orientations) and the nationalist sector in the Brazilian army, both supporting the idea of building an important sector of science and technology as an instrument for promoting the country's strategic interests.

Under the framework created by the nationalistic approach to science and technology policies, the main Brazilian investment bank—the government-owned Banco Nacional de Desenvolvimento Econômico—established a strong program to support technological development. The success of the fund created pressures for it to be institutionalized into a new specialized agency, the Financiadora de Estudos e Projetos, which was in charge of a National Fund for the Development of Science and Technology, entitled to a permanent share of the federal budget. In 1975 the small Conselho Nacional de Pesquisa (National Research Council) was reformed and transformed into a new and larger Conselho Nacional de Desenvolvimento Científico e tecnológico (National Council for Scientific and Technological Development [CNPq]), placed under control of the Ministry of Planning, then an important branch of the Brazilian government.

The 1970s were years of economic expansion, in which the Brazilian economy grew at annual rates of 7 to 10 percent. These new agencies had funds to spend, as well as a flexible and modern bureaucracy not constrained by the rigid controls one found in other governmental offices. Their first attempts were directed toward stimulating private and public firms to invest in technological development. But these initiatives were mostly doomed to fail due to the firms' lack of interest in investing in such a risky enterprise, being placed, as they were, in a highly protected environment created by the macroeconomic import substitution policies. The agencies then turned their attention toward the informal research environments to be found in some of the most prestigious universities, where some scientific tradition was in place.

With such support, postgraduate education in Brazil grew at a rapid pace. In 1965, when postgraduate studies where recognized, the National Education Council accredited 38 postgraduate programs: 27 as master's degrees and 11 as doctoral programs. Ten years later, in 1975, there were already 429 MA programs and 149 doctoral programs. Since the beginning of 2000, the number of students attending a graduate program, either at the master's or doctoral level, increased 82 percent, going from 94,400 to 172,000 students. In the last decade, the country graduated more than 86,000 doctors and more than 338,000 masters.

The Quest for Financial Autonomy

While the country's new Constitution of 1988 granted expanded autonomy for universities in Brazil, and the Education Law of 1997 reinforced the notion of university's autonomy in research and pedagogic realms, in reality, this autonomy is very limited. In the federal level, financial autonomy is nonexistent. Universities' budgets are covered by resources coming from the Ministry of Education that tend to reproduce the historical budget pattern. Any extra money needed for covering new initiatives or improving infrastructure should be negotiated with the Ministry of Education and the powerful Secretary for Higher Education. Staff salaries (including academic ones) are paid directly by the Federal Ministry of Planning. Under this picture, it comes as no surprise that the de facto autonomy of federal universities is strongly restricted. Even when dealing with the more powerful and better-established old universities that are more active in research and graduate education, the Ministry of Education has strong leverage to impose its own view.

The only exception in this general picture comes from the state of São Paulo. In 1987 the state of São Paulo's public universities[3] reached a comfortable situation of ample and unrestricted autonomy. From that year on, the three universities had guaranteed access to 8 percent of the major state revenue, a tax applied to all commercial or service transaction occurred inside the state.[4] The autonomy then granted to São Paulo state universities resulted from a long and aggressive strike that united the academic staff and employees' unions from the three universities, as well as the student movements. From the unions' and university authorities' point of view, achieving financial autonomy represented the fulfillment of more than a decade of struggles for independency from political influence. From the point of view of the government, the agreement was a price to pay in order to stop the increasing political costs created by the constant attritions between universities and government, usually escalated by the intense coverage they received in the media.

Since then, these resources have been automatically transferred to the universities' administrations, without any kind of restriction. At that time, the proportional share to which each university was entitled was defined in a meeting between the three universities' rectors and the governor. The agreement then reached was that the proportional commitment of state revenues to the universities should replicate the proportion observed in the previous year (including investments then made in infrastructure). This pact is still in effect.

Financial autonomy had a strong impact on the dynamics of the São Paulo universities and represented a push for consolidating their leadership among elite research universities in Brazil. Internally, it reinforced budgetary responsibility and allowed for long-term planning, which improved the academic profession, research infrastructure, and support for research and graduate training, which, in turn, attracted the more dynamic and research-oriented academics in Brazil. Since the beginning of the

1990s, holding a PhD has been a requirement for any candidate who applies for the academic staff in these universities.

Financial autonomy is the differential explanation of the relative success of the São Paulo universities in the international ranks of universities worldwide. The University of São Paulo is the only Brazilian university classified among the top 150 by the journal *Times Higher Education* (THE). The University of Campinas (UNICAMP) is among the top 200, and is classified among the top 20 in the 2012 THE's ranking of new universities. All three state-owned universities are also well positioned in the Shanghai Academic Ranking of World Universities.

Present and Future Challenges

Taken in perspective, the experience of building up research universities in Brazil was relatively successful. Nevertheless, the whole process faces some hindrances that have become more visible in the last decade with the change in the international higher education landscape.

Some of the problems come from the very success of graduate evaluation, as it is carried out by CAPES. In spite of its positive aspects, CAPES evaluation had some hindrances that became more and more apparent as time went by. The small size of the Brazilian scientific community and the visibility of the peer committees' work created unavoidable parochial pressures. One consequence was grade inflation (Castro & Soares 1986). In 1996, four in every five programs were placed in the two highest ranks, A or B, which meant that the CAPES evaluation was quickly losing any discriminating role.

Reacting to this situation, CAPES authorities established in 1998 a new model for program evaluation. This new model preserved the authority of the peer committees, but adopted more formal rules for evaluation. It reinforced the adoption of some fixed parameters for all fields of knowledge, stressing faculty academic background and research performance as measured by their publishing patterns; extended the periodicity of evaluation from two to three years; adopted a more comprehensive procedure, evaluating master's and doctoral programs together, instead of evaluating each program per se; and adopted a scale of 7 points (instead of 5), where the ranks of 6 and 7 are restricted to programs offering doctoral degrees that could be qualified as good or excellent by international standards, and establishing that 3 was the lowest acceptable rank for successfully accrediting a postgraduate program.

While the reform of CAPES procedures succeeded in imposing new and more stringent requirements for graduate education, it has done so by reducing the autonomy of peer evaluation and reinforcing the weight of formal procedures. The new uniform parameters applied to all fields opened a way for stronger political influence from the agency's bureaucracy in the whole procedure, while at the same time, reducing its tolerance to new experimental or alternative models of graduate education. In the new model, evaluation has curbed some of the more dynamic experiences in graduate education (Silva & Proença, 2012), especially in those new emerging areas that could be characterized by transdisciplinarity and new dynamics of knowledge production (Gibbons et al., 1994; Bonaccorsi & Vargas, 2007).

Another major challenge facing these universities is posed by the strong pressures coming from Brazilian society and government for an accelerated expansion of the share of public universities in the overall country's supply of places for undergraduate study. In the past, the standard description of the differences between the public and private institutions used to be as follows: Public higher education in Brazil was free from tuition, most courses were provided during the day, and faculty members were civil servants with full-time contracts. To be admitted, students had to pass very competitive entrance examinations. Private institutions, on the other hand, charged tuition, most of the instruction was given in the evenings, and admission was easy. Most of the faculty worked part time and had no career plans or job security. The new social pact that sustained the transition to democracy in Brazil in the 1990s reinforced the perception of the illegitimacy of this situation where the poor, because of the deficiencies of public primary and secondary education, are forced to pay, while the rich have access to higher education for free. This situation created strong pressures for opening access to public higher education and prompted the government to launch programs aiming to quickly expand enrollments at undergraduate level in the federal universities and impose quota programs to increase the presence of minorities in the universities' student bodies.[5] These programs created strong pressures for a rapid process of massification of the public sector, which may, in the long run, jeopardize the research profile of the best federal universities.

The second challenge comes from the recent success of the country in building a large, strong graduate layer inside higher education. Since the mid-1980s, the growth of graduate education in all areas has been stimulated following a reasoning that stressed the economy of scale of having all academics trained domestically instead of developing big programs for sending students abroad for their graduate studies. This created a very peculiar dynamic inside Brazilian graduate education that strongly reinforced its insulation from external influences. Thus, comparing the international involvement of Brazilian academics with teaching responsibilities at the doctoral level with academics with the same profile in the other 17 countries that were included in the CAP project (Figure 8.1), the degree of insulation experienced by the elite of the Brazilian academics is surprising. While almost 20 percent of all academics with teaching responsibilities in Brazil have no relevant interaction with peers abroad, for another 20 percent, the interaction is restricted to some publication abroad. At the other extreme, only a bit more than 10 percent of these academics reported a full portfolio of interaction with peers abroad, including research partnerships, access to international funds for research, and co-authoring publications with colleagues from abroad.

FIGURE 8.1: INTERNATIONAL ACTIVITY OF ACADEMICS WITH TEACHING RESPONSIBILITIES AT DOCTORAL LEVEL IN 18 COUNTRIES

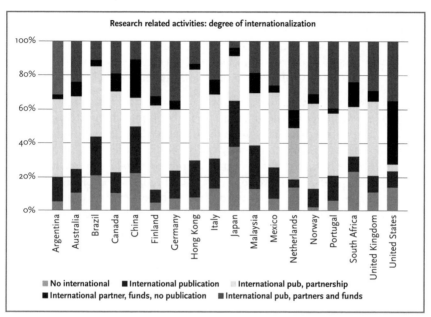

In July 2011, the Brazilian government drastically changed this orientation, launching the Brazil Scientific Mobility Program, a multiyear initiative to send 75,000 fully funded Brazilian students abroad for training in the science, technology, engineering, and math (STEM) fields, with an additional 26,000 scholarships expected to be funded by the private sector. It is early for a full evaluation of the program's impact on the Brazilian higher education landscape. The first reports tend to stress problems in finding candidates with adequate profiles (especially English proficiency) to fill all the scholarships offered in the program. Another issue raised is related to the narrow coverage of the program in terms of fields. In fact, most social sciences, arts, and humanities are left out of the program, and critics point out that these are the areas where parochial tendencies are more pronounced, and where such a program could have most relevant impact. Finally, some raise worries regarding the ability of the agencies in charge of these programs to fully supervise the use of the fellowships in order to ensure that the students really go to the best training alternatives. While the choice of only accepting applications for universities listed in the top positions of the best known international ranks is an answer to the last problem, it may create artificial restrictions that can prevent students from having access to the best training options in some selected areas, where good training options are offered in specialized institutions.

Last but not least, there is the challenge of public universities' governance. One of the legacies of the country's struggle for democracy in the 1980s is the almost unchallenged paradigm of "democratic governance" as the best model of governance for public universities. The term "democratic governance" refers to the arrangement whereby institutional authorities are chosen in open elections involving all perceived relevant forces inside the university: academics, students, and employees.

While the model seems to accommodate most of the internal tensions, it frequently gives rise to veto coalitions that strongly oppose change, experimentation, and more competitive dynamics inside the university. At the same time, this governance model, in the absence of formal oversight bodies representing external interest, tends to close the university's decision-making processes to all external influences and to magnify the relevance of the vested interests of internal stakeholders. In this framework, one of the main roles of institution's authorities is to serve as a buffer between the political exigencies posed by the government and the interests sustained by the main internal forces.

Again, there are some differences in the way democratic governance works inside research universities and regional universities. As Balbachevsky and Schwartzman (2011) have shown, in the former settings, collegiate arrangements tend to be more active. In the latter settings, collegiate arrangements are less prevalent and in many decision areas they are surpassed by more personal ways in which faculty as individuals express their interests, alongside other internal constituencies.

Conclusion

This chapter has presented an account of the processes that supported growth and differentiation inside the Brazilian public sector, creating the conditions for the development of a group of universities that can be described as real research universities. As argued here, nurturing such institutions was an unintended consequence of the policies directed at building up and protecting graduate education and in support of science adopted in the 1970s, in order to further the strategic goal of strengthening national research capabilities for national development. The institutional differentiation described here was never acknowledged by Brazilian law, practice, or policy. In the past the fiction of an undifferentiated public sector, comprised of universities equally dedicated to research, teaching, and extension, was beneficial to all public institutions.

This is not true anymore. The more unstable and competitive international environment is knocking at the door of Brazilian universities, thanks to the forced comparison brought by the visibility of international rankings and the experiences with other academic cultures brought by a new generation of students that are coming home from their studies and internships abroad. These new dynamics add new cross-pressures to institutions that are already stressed by the changes in the demands posed by government. How Brazilian research universities will fare in the turbulences of the new environment is an open question.

NOTES

[1] Brazil, like all Latin American countries, adopted the continental model of higher education in which undergraduate training is supposed to result in a bachelor's degree, which certifies the completion of the first cycle of higher education and, at the same time, accredits the holder as a full-fledged professional, entitled to exercise his or her profession.

[2] For an overview of the Brazilian graduate education, see Balbachevsky (2004), Balbachevsky & Schwartzman (2010), and CGEE (2010).

[3] In Brazil, the federative arrangement allows the state (provincial) governments to organize their own higher education systems that run parallel to the federal system and the private system. State universities are the sole responsibility of the state-level government and are not subject to the Ministry of Education's regulations or evaluation (as is the case of federal and private universities). The state of São Paulo, the richest and most dynamic economy in Brazil, created three universities since 1932: The University of São Paulo, the State University of São Paulo "Júlio de Mesquita," and the State University of Campinas (UNICAMP). These three universities are considered among the best universities in Brazil, with strong commitment to graduate education and research. Since the 1960s, research and graduate education at these universities have been supported by contributions from federal funds as well as the state-level Science Foundation (FAPESP). By law, FAPESP is entitled to 1 percent of all state revenues, and also by law, the administrative costs of FAPESP cannot be more than 5 percent of its resources. Thus, most of its resources are used to support research projects, going directly to researchers and graduate students.

[4] This proportion rose to 9.6 percent in 1994, after a strong strike inside the universities. It has been frozen since then, but since state revenues have increased in real terms, the universities never lack support for their expenses.

[5] In October 2012 the federal government enacted a law approved by the congress that reserves 50 percent of the entries at federal universities to students from poor families, minorities, and those who attended all primary and secondary education in public schools.

REFERENCES

Balbachevsky, E. (2000). *A profissão acadêmica no Brasil: As múltiplas facetas do nosso sistema de ensino superior.* Brasília, Brazil: FUNADESP.

Balbachevsky, E. (2004). Graduate education: Emerging challenges to a successful policy. In C. Broock, S. Schwartzman (Eds.), *The challenges of education in Brazil* (pp. 209–228). Oxford: Symposium Books.

Balbachevsky, E. (2011). Academic careers in Brazil: The legacy of the past. *Journal of the Professoriate, 5*(2), 95–121.

Balbachevsky, E., & Schwartzman, S. (2010). The graduate foundations of research in Brazil. *Higher Education Forum, 7*(1), 85–100.

Balbachevsky, E., & Schwartzman, S. (2011). Brazil: Diverse experiences in institutional governance in the public and private sectors. In W. Locke, W. Cummings, & D. Fisher (Eds.), *Changing governance and management in higher education: The perspectives of academy* (pp. 35–56). Dordrecht, The Netherlands: Springer, 2011.

Bonaccorsi, A., & Vargas, J. (2007). *Proliferation dynamics in emerging sciences.* Paper presented in PRIME Workshop on Nanodistricts, Grenoble, France, 7–9 Septembro de 2006, na Conferencia "Science and its publics," Munich, 24–25 June 2007. Retrieved from http://citeseerx.ist.psu.edu/viewdoc/download?doi=10.1.1.121.7555&rep=rep1&type=pdf

Castro, C., & Soares, G. A. D. (1986). As avaliações da Capes. In S. Schwartzman & C. Castro. (Eds.), *Pesquisa universitária em questão* (pp. 190–224). São Paulo, Brazil: Editora da UNICAMP.

CGEE. (2010). *Doutores 2010: Estudos da demografia da base técnico-científica brasileira.* Brasília: CGEE.

Coutinho, M. (1996). Ecology and environmental science in Brazilian higher education; Graduate programs, research and intellectual identity. *NUPES, Documentos de Trabalho, 6.*

Durhan, E. R. (1998). Uma política para o ensino superior brasileiro: Diagnóstico e proposta. *Documentos de Trabalho NUPES 1/98.* São Paulo, Brazil: Universidade de São Paulo.

Fulton, O., & Trow, M. (1975). Research activity in American higher education. In M. Trow (Ed.), *Teachers and students: Aspects of American higher education* (pp. 39–63). New York, NY: McGraw-Hill.

Gibbons, M., Limonges, C., Nowotny, H., Schwartzman, S. Scott, P., & Trow, M. (1994). *The new production of knowledge.* Thousand Oaks, CA: Sage.

INEP. (2011). Censo da educação superior 2010, Resumo técnico. Brasília: Ministério da Educação, INEP. Retrieved from http://download.inep.gov.br/educacao_superior/censo_superior/resumo_tecnico/resumo_tecnico_censo_educaca o_superior_2010.pdf

Klein, L. (1992). Política e políticas de ensino superior no Brasil: 1970–1990. *Documento de Trabalho NUPES 2/92.* São Paulo, Brazil: Universidade de São Paulo.

Silva, E. R. P., & Proença, R. (2012). *Os indicadores CAPES na Engenharia arriscam a perda da capacidade de projeto do Brasil.* Retrieved from https://sites.google.com/site/tudoeheuristica/home

Schwartzman, J. (1993). Universidades federais no Brasil: Uma avaliação de suas trajetórias—décadas de 70 e 80. *Documento de Trabalho NUPES 4/93.* São Paulo, Brazil: Universidade de São Paulo.

Schwartzman, S. (1991). *A space for science: The development of the scientific community in Brazil.* University Park: Pennsylvania State University Press. Retrieved from http://www.schwartzman.org.br/simon/space/summary.htm

Schwartzman, S., & Balbachevsky, E. (1997). The academic profession in Brazil. In P. G. Altbach (Ed.) *The international academic profession: Portraits of fourteen countries* (pp. 231–278). Princeton, NJ: The Carnegie Foundation for the Advancement of Teaching.

Velloso, J. (1987). Política educacional e recursos para o ensino: O salário-educação e a universidade federal. *Caderno de Pesquisa*, maio 1987, 3–28.

Chapter Nine

THE BRAZIL SCIENTIFIC MOBILITY PROGRAM: ADVANCING INNOVATION, COMPETITIVENESS, AND BUSINESS LEADERSHIP

Interview with Aloizio Mercadante, Minister of Education, Government of Brazil
Conducted by Allan E. Goodman, President and CEO, IIE

What are the primary goals that President Dilma Rousseff and your office have set for higher education in Brazil?

One of Brazil's primary goals is to grant more Brazilians access to undergraduate courses and higher education, which until recently was only for the elite. Actions aimed at increasing the number of vacancies in public and private higher education networks, as well as for vocational and technological education, will ensure better diversity in terms of access to undergraduate courses.

In higher education, Brazil has seen an increase in the enrollment of young people between the ages of 18 and 24 from 7.3 percent in 2000 to 14.4 percent in 2009. Despite these advances, Brazil needs to continue to ensure that its population reaches a high level of education. The National Education Plan (PNE) was enacted to increase the gross and net enrollment rates in higher education. Through

IIE/AIFS Foundation Global Education Research Reports
LATIN AMERICA'S NEW KNOWLEDGE ECONOMY: HIGHER EDUCATION, GOVERNMENT, AND INTERNATIONAL COLLABORATION

133

this plan, we are targeting a net enrollment increase of 30 percent of the young people aged between 18 and 24, or over four million students, by the year 2020.

By 2021, Brazil's national goal is to have a federal university campus in every town with over 100,000 inhabitants and a campus of a federal institute of education, science and technology in towns with over 50,000 people.

The Brazil Scientific Mobility Program provides scholarships to undergraduate and graduate students from Brazil for study in the United States and other countries, with a preference given to students in the science, technology, engineering, and mathematics (STEM) fields. Could you talk about the genesis of this program, and its initial motivations and ambitions?

The program is a bold, integrated initiative for national development. The aim is to provide 75,000 scholarships for Brazilian students to study abroad with government funding by 2015, so that our best undergraduate and graduate students, as well as researchers, may engage with the world's best universities, where innovation, entrepreneurship, and competitiveness are already the standard. The scholarships will be provided in multiple formats, including sandwich-undergraduate, vocational, and technological education, and sandwich-doctorate, full-doctorate, and postdoctorate scholarships.

In addition, the program aims to attract foreign researchers who want to live and research in Brazil, and to create opportunity for researchers from companies to go abroad for expert training. The participation of large national companies in the program is strategic, as together they may contribute at least another 26,000 scholarships abroad.

How did the Brazil Scientific Mobility Program emerge as the best course of action? What other interventions and strategies were under consideration?

The program was developed directly in response to Brazil's need to catch up in global education and scientific knowledge production. The program promotes the consolidation, expansion, and internationalization of science, technology, and innovation, and Brazilian competitiveness through the exchange and international mobility of students, professors, and researchers.

What sort of outcomes is the government of Brazil striving for with the Scientific Mobility Program, and how will you measure success? What skills are you hoping the students who participate in the program will bring back to Brazil?

Through the program, the federal government intends to invest in the development of highly qualified personnel with the necessary abilities and skills for advancing the economy of knowledge, with a focus on great national challenges, particularly in engineering and other technological areas. The goal is to empower Brazilian students to apply what they have studied, learned, and researched in priority areas at the world's best universities back home. Overall, we aim to create the human resources necessary for long-term national development.

You were most recently the Minister for Science, Technology, and Innovation in Brazil. How will the Scientific Mobility Program help advance scientific innovation, entrepreneurship, and workforce development in the country?

Developing education and science is one of Brazil's greatest challenges. The program will drive innovation because it focuses on the areas of engineering, technology, and basic sciences. It is critical for Brazil to prepare for societal and knowledge-related challenges. The government aims to increase the country's level of competitiveness and contribute so that small and medium-sized enterprises can take a technological leap. The expectation is for the program to bring economic growth to Brazil.

What measures is the government of Brazil considering to ensure that the country retains newly trained knowledge workers?

Brazil still has a shortage of skilled labor opportunities that will allow students with high-level training to become professionals that stand out in their fields. In light of the economic growth currently experienced in the country, job opportunities will grow and become attractive to new graduates. In addition, the program aims to attract young scientific talents and highly qualified researchers from abroad to work in Brazil.

What role do you see higher education playing in Brazil's affairs more broadly, specifically in the bilateral relationship between Brazil and the United States?

Brazil's partnerships with foreign higher education institutions represent an important opportunity for all professors and students involved and allow for the strengthening of relationships between countries. In addition, these partnerships contribute to providing more visibility to the academic and scientific research done in Brazil through collaboration and joint research projects with foreign institutions and partners.

The Brazilian government wants more American universities to accept Brazilian scholarship students. Currently, 791 Brazilian scholarship holders are already studying in the United States.[1] Our goal is for approximately one-fifth of the scholarship holders to study in the United States.

The Brazil Scientific Mobility Undergraduate Program in the United States[2]

EDWARD MONKS, IIE

In July 2011, Brazilian President Dilma Rousseff announced the creation of a new scholarship program known as *Ciência sem Fronteiras,* a multiyear initiative to send 75,000 fully funded Brazilian students abroad for training in the science, technology, engineering, and math (STEM) fields, with an additional 26,000 scholarships expected to be funded by the private sector. This initiative is coordinated jointly by the Brazilian Ministry of Science and Technology's National Council for Scientific and Technological Development (CNPq) and the Ministry of Education's Federal Agency for the Support and Evaluation of Graduate Education (CAPES).

The program was created to promote scientific research, invest and fund educational resources within Brazil and outside of the country, increase international cooperation in science and technology, and initiate and engage students in a global dialogue through international education. Scholarships are awarded for study in more than 12 countries including Australia, Belgium, Canada, France, Germany, Italy, the Netherlands, Portugal, South Korea, Spain, the United Kingdom, and the United States. The United States currently hosts the largest number of students, followed by France, Portugal, and Spain (see Table 9.1).

TABLE 9.1: NUMBER OF CIÊNCIA SEM FRONTEIRAS SCHOLARSHIPS AWARDED

Country	CNPq	CAPES	Total
United States	2,110	1,954	4,064
France	1,257	1,759	3,016
Portugal	1,986		1,986
Spain	1,575		1,575
Germany	565	531	1,096
United Kingdom	495	479	974
Canada	902	71	973
Italy	443	285	728
Australia	264		264
Netherlands	182		182
Note: The numbers in this table reflect scholarships awarded, and do not necessarily correspond to enrollments. The scholarship program in Australia, the Netherlands, Portugal, and Spain is coordinated by CNPq only.			

Source: CAPES and CNPq

The program offers scholarships to Brazilians in five different categories, including undergraduate, visiting doctoral studies, full PhD degrees, postdoctoral training, and specialized training in industry (see Table 9.2 for complete breakdown). The initiative also offers fellowships to young scientists and visiting researchers from other countries to study or conduct research in Brazil.

TABLE 9.2: AWARD CATEGORIES AND ANTICIPATED NUMBER OF SCHOLARSHIPS

Category	Duration	Number of Scholarships
Undergraduate study abroad	6–12 months (up to 15 months if language training included)	27,100
Visiting doctoral studies	3–12 months	24,600
Full PhD degrees	4 years	9,790
Postdoctoral training	6–12 months (renewable to 24 months)	11,560
Talented young scientists (to Brazil)	Up to 3 years	860
Specialized training in industry	4–12 months	700
Special visiting researcher (to Brazil)	At least 1 month per year for at least 3 years	390
Total		75,000

Source: Capes and CNPq

CAPES partnered with the Institute of International Education (IIE) in August 2011 to administer the undergraduate program in the United States, which allows students to complete up to one year of nondegree study, in addition to an academic training or internship component. CNPq entered into the partnership in March of 2012.

In the undergraduate program, all candidates must first be nominated by their Brazilian university, and their participation must be approved by CAPES or CNPq. The candidates are further reviewed by IIE and submitted for placement to one of the participating U.S. higher education institutions. The final decision to accept a student in the program is made by the participating U.S. host campus.

Students who do not meet the minimum TOEFL requirement for immediate academic placement but otherwise qualify are provided intensive English language training for six to eight weeks and then transition to an academic program. The Institute of International Education's pre-academic training department handles the placement of these students in more than 30 Intensive English Language Programs across the country.

A recent report published by IIE, *The Brazil Scientific Mobility Undergraduate Program in the United States: A New Phase in U.S.-Brazil Educational Exchange*, provides an overview of the Brazil Scientific Mobility Undergraduate Program[3] in the United States and presents a snapshot of current trends.

Report Highlights

- As of the fall 2012 semester, 1,954 Brazilian undergraduate scholarship students have been placed at 238 U.S. host institutions in 46 U.S. states. The program is projected to enroll 2,500 students per academic year for the next five years of the program.

- Nearly three-fourths (71 percent) of the students are enrolled in engineering and computer science courses, specifically in mechanical engineering, electrical engineering, computer sciences, industrial engineering, and chemical engineering.

- Female students on this program are more likely to major in medical fields or the hard sciences than their male counterparts.

- The top five U.S. host states are California, New York, Michigan, Illinois, and Ohio.

- About one-third (31 percent) of the scholarship students participated in academic training, including internships, which takes place during the summer months between semesters or at the conclusion of their two academic terms. The private sector has been eager to provide internship placement, and IIE has identified nearly 100 corporate partners/internship hosts so far.

NOTES

[1] Since this interview was conducted in early 2012, the number has risen to approximately 2,000 students.

[2] This article is an excerpt from a report, *The Brazil Scientific Mobility Undergraduate Program in the United States: A New Phase in U.S.-Brazil Educational Exchange*, published in October 2012 by the Institute of International Education. The full report is available at www.iie.org/brazilreport.

[3] The Brazil Scientific Mobility program was formerly known as Brazil Science Without Borders.

Appendix

Broadening Opportunities for Higher Education Exchange in Latin America and the Caribbean: IIE's Role and Work in the Region

Neshani Jani and Jonah Kokodyniak, IIE

Throughout its history, the Institute of International Education (IIE) has been a leader in developing scholarship, exchange, and training programs for Latin America and the Caribbean, with an emphasis on programs that strengthen academic ties between the people of the U.S. and countries in the Western Hemisphere. In the early 1930s, IIE established a Latin America Division at its New York headquarters. It opened its Latin America regional office in Mexico City in 1974.

Since then, the Institute's work in the Western Hemisphere has grown to include a number of dynamic initiatives related to higher education, scholarship, and fellowship programs, promoting study abroad, workforce and professional development, institutional partnership building, educational advising, and English language testing.

Our programs build leadership skills and enhance the capacity of individuals and organizations to address local and global challenges. We connect students and professionals with peers and colleagues around the world and prepare them for leadership in fields and professions essential to advancing peace and prosperity for all.

To cite a few examples of this work, in recent years, IIE has launched partnerships with the government of Brazil, ExxonMobil, NYU Abu Dhabi, and the Alcoa Foundation to build global talent in the region, undertake new research, develop strategic higher education links, and engage leaders in dialogue on the role of higher education institutions as incubators of innovation, workforce development, and international discourse.

The following sections provide a brief overview of the highlights and impacts of the programs implemented by the Institute's offices and networks, including IIE's Latin America Regional Office, based in Mexico City.

Promoting Mutual Understanding: Scholar and Student Exchange Programs

The Fulbright Program enables participants from diverse cultural, ethnic, and economic backgrounds to create ties of understanding and respect between the United States and other countries. The program is sponsored by the Bureau of Educational and Cultural Affairs (ECA) of the U.S. Department of State, with additional funding from foreign governments, higher education institutions, private sector partners, and donors. IIE and its Council for International Exchange of Scholars (CIES) have been proud partners in the Fulbright Program since its inception in 1946. Last year, the Fulbright Student Program granted nearly 180 awards for Americans to study in Latin America and the Caribbean and more than 660 awards to Foreign Fulbright students from the region to pursue studies in the United States. This past year the Fulbright Scholar Program made over 50 grants to U.S. scholars to teach and conduct research in Latin America and the Caribbean; in addition, nearly 30 visiting scholars and specialists came to the United States from the region.

A component of the Fulbright Student Program, the Foreign Language Teaching Assistant (FLTA) Program supported nearly 60 native Spanish- and Portuguese-speaking teaching assistants from the region to teach and serve as cultural ambassadors at higher education institutions across the United States. The English Teaching Assistantship (ETA) places U.S. Fulbrighters in classrooms abroad to assist teachers of English to non-native-English speakers. English teaching assistants help teach the English language while serving as cultural ambassadors for U.S. culture. Last year, nearly 120 ETAs traveled to Latin America through the Fulbright Student Program.

The Fulbright Scholar Program recently launched the Regional Network for Applied Research (NEXUS) Program in Buenos Aires, Argentina. The NEXUS initiative brings together 20 applied scholars and midcareer researchers from the United States and nine other Western Hemisphere nations (Canada, Mexico, Jamaica, Colombia, Ecuador, Brazil, Uruguay, Argentina, and Chile) for a series of seminars and a yearlong Fulbright scholarly exchange. These scholars are focusing on harnessing innovative strategies and technologies to bring about practical solutions to real-world challenges in renewable energy, climate change, public health, and sustainable growth.

The Hubert H. Humphrey Fellowship Program, funded by the Bureau of Educational and Cultural Affairs of the U.S. Department of State, provides a year of professional enrichment in the United States for experienced professionals from designated countries, including many in Latin America and the Caribbean. This past year, the program hosted nearly 40 fellows from the Western Hemisphere and, to date, has welcomed almost 800 alumni from the region.

Promoting Study Abroad in the Region

To prepare students for an increasingly global economy and interdependent world, IIE has made it a priority to expand opportunities for diverse American students to study abroad and to diversify the regions in which they study. Key to this is a commitment to increasing study abroad to Latin America, especially among U.S. students from underrepresented backgrounds and institutions.

Central to achieving these goals is the Benjamin A. Gilman International Scholarship Program, which enables outstanding undergraduate students with financial need to study outside of the United States. Administered on behalf of the U.S. Department of State, the Gilman Program has made a dramatic impact in this area by awarding more than 10,650 scholarships since its inception in 2001. Nearly 20 percent of Gilman recipients study abroad in Latin America, in countries such as Argentina, Chile, Costa Rica, and Mexico.

Having citizens who are more proficient in the world's languages and cultures is critical to U.S. interests. With funding from the National Security Education Program, the Boren Scholarships and Fellowships provide U.S. undergraduate and graduate students with opportunities to focus on geographic areas, languages, and fields of study deemed critical to U.S. national security. The program gives preference to applicants planning to study in one of the following countries in Latin America and the Caribbean: Argentina, Brazil, Chile, Colombia, Cuba, El Salvador, Guatemala, Haiti, Honduras, Mexico, Nicaragua, Panama, Peru, and Venezuela.

IIE also promotes study abroad programs in Latin America through the IIEPassport Study Abroad Directory and the online search engine www.IIEPassport.org, which include detailed information on more than 9,500 study abroad programs.

Managing Scholarship Programs

IIE provides scholarships to talented individuals from around the world to study abroad in specialized fields that will build a skilled workforce in their home countries and contribute to local community development. Through a wide variety of educational programs sponsored by the U.S. government, corporations, foundations, and foreign governments, the Institute helps to place more than 3,000 Latin American undergraduates and graduates at colleges and universities in the United States and 175 other countries.

Recently, IIE partnered with the Brazilian government to promote scientific research and increase international cooperation in science and technology through the Brazil Scientific Mobility Program. In the first phase of the program, IIE is administering scholarships for undergraduate students from Brazil for one year of study at colleges and universities in the United States. Scholarships are given primarily to students in the science, technology, engineering, and mathematics fields and include an internship opportunity at leading corporations.

IIE also administers the GE Foundation Scholar-Leaders Program, which supports outstanding students who are financially disadvantaged or are underrepresented in higher education geographically, ethnically, or by gender in academic institutions in 14 countries around the world. The program creates opportunities for students to realize their potential through practical training and leadership development and includes a Western Hemisphere component that provides grants for Mexican, Brazilian, Canadian, and U.S. students studying industrial, mechanical, and systems engineering or business administration. In addition, IIE recently launched the Cargill Global Scholars Program, which will provide financial support, leadership development, and enrichment opportunities to nearly 200 talented and high-performing undergraduate students in five countries, including Brazil.

Through the Inter-American Foundation Grassroots Development Fellowships, IIE supports doctoral students from the United States and Latin America who are currently studying at U.S. universities and are pursuing yearlong field dissertation research on grassroots development topics across Latin America and the Caribbean. After fellows finish their fieldwork, IIE assists with the dissemination of their research findings to the development community.

The impact that scholarship programs have on development in the region is evident. For example, 82 percent of alumni in the Ford Foundation International Fellowships Program (IFP), which placed fellowship candidates from the developing world into universities in the United States and throughout the Americas, are engaging in economic, social justice, and development work in their home countries. More than 1,000 IFP Fellows from Brazil, Chile, Guatemala, Mexico, and Peru have earned graduate degrees through the program, and 80 percent of these fellows are indigenous or afro-descendant. From 1989 to 2008, IIE established the Regional Program for Graduate Fellowships in the Social Sciences, funded by the Ford, Hewlett, and Macarthur Foundations, in order to support students, professors, and researchers in Mexico and Central America strengthen the impact of social sciences in these countries. The program developed more than 1,000 leaders in the public and private sectors across the region.

Professional Development

IIE has expertise in designing innovative programs that include short-term seminars, workshops, extended programs, and international exchange opportunities that improve the ability of students, professionals, and youth to develop their full potential and actively contribute to their communities. The long- and short-term training programs arranged by the Institute connect students and professionals with peers and colleagues around the world to gain the skills and international perspectives they will need to forge solutions to global challenges.

IIE makes it possible for U.S. teachers to bring a new awareness of global issues home to their students. Professional study tours enable teachers to travel overseas to learn about other cultures, interact with educators from host countries, and build links with host institutions in order to deepen their students' knowledge of the world. Through the Toyota International Teacher Program sponsored by Toyota Motor Sales, U.S.A., 29 secondary educators traveled to the Galapagos Islands and 25 went to Costa Rica to study environmental stewardship from biological and ecological perspectives. Back home, they engaged their students in developing solutions to local and global environmental problems.

Another example is the USAID-sponsored Emerging Markets Development Advisers Program (EMDAP), which recruits recent graduates of U.S. master's programs in business, development studies, and related fields to provide management assistance as advisers to small and medium-sized enterprises in developing nations. In Latin America and the Caribbean, IIE has placed advisers in Chile, Barbados, the Dominican Republic, Ecuador, Guatemala, Guyana, Haiti, Mexico, Nicaragua, Panama, and Peru.

Building Partnerships

IIE's Center for International Partnerships (CIP) assists higher education institutions in developing partnerships around the world through a range of training programs, including the International Academic Partnership Program (IAPP)—a yearlong program for U.S. campuses focused on implementing and sustaining partnerships with higher education institutions in emerging international academic hubs such as Brazil, China, India, Indonesia, and Myanmar.

As the Brazilian economy continues to grow and Brazil expands its world reach, higher education linkages will become even more important in the relationship between the United States and Brazil. Now in its second phase, IAPP Brazil seeks to increase those institutional partnerships by helping U.S. institutions navigate the Brazilian higher education system, think critically about a strategic partnership plan, and access the tools and resources necessary to make informed decisions.

Educational Advising and English for Academic Opportunity

IIE is also committed to expanding access to U.S. higher education and English language training across Latin America and the Caribbean. The EducationUSA advising staff based at IIE's Mexico City office, respond to approximately 80,000 annual requests for information from students and professionals throughout the country who are interested in studying in the United States. IIE also has three Regional Educational Advising Coordinators in Latin America, based in Mexico, Peru, and Brazil. Both programs are administered on behalf of the U.S. Department of State.

English language skills are critical for opening doors to academic opportunity in the region. IIE's work in this area includes administration of the second largest TOEFL Institutional Testing Programs in the world and the TOEFL junior test, collaboration with the U.S. Department of State in managing the English Access Micro Scholarship Program for marginalized students, and testing and training of English language teachers and supervisors.

About the Contributors

Jorge Balán is a senior research scholar and adjunct professor at the School of International and Public Affairs, Columbia University. He was a professor at the University of Buenos Aires (UBA) until 1997, when he joined the Ford Foundation in New York as a senior program officer for higher education. A book on research universities in Asia and Latin America, edited by Balán and Philip Altbach (Johns Hopkins University Press), was translated into several languages, and his most recent piece on research universities in Latin America appeared in the fall 2012 edition of the journal *Social Research*. He holds an undergraduate degree from UBA and a PhD from The University of Texas at Austin, both in sociology.

Elizabeth Balbachevsky is associate professor at the Department of Political Science at the University of São Paulo, Brazil, deputy director of the university's Center for Public Policy Research, and fellow at the Higher Education Group in the Center for Advanced Studies at University of Campinas. She was a Fulbright New Century Scholar in 2005–2006 and an Erasmus Mundus Scholar at the European Master's in Higher Education Programme (2009). Balbachevsky's publications include "Brazil: Diverse Experience in Institutional Governance in the Public and Private Sectors" in *Changing Governance and Management in Higher Education: The Perspectives of the Academy* and "Incentives and Obstacles to Academic Entrepreneurship" in *University and Development in Latin America: Successful Experiences of Research Centers.*

Raisa Belyavina is a senior research officer with the Center for Academic Mobility Research at the Institute of International Education. She manages Project Atlas, an initiative to collect and disseminate timely data on global student mobility. Prior to joining IIE, Belyavina worked in education domestically and internationally. Most recently, she conducted research in Armenia for UNICEF. Belyavina was on a Fulbright Fellowship in Korea in 2008 and has a BA in political science and an MA in international education, both from Columbia University.

Andrés Bernasconi is a professor of higher education at the Pontificia Universidad Católica de Chile and a research associate at its Center for Research of Educational Policy and Practice. Previously, he served as dean and provost in other universities. Bernasconi specializes in higher education policy and management, with a regional focus in Latin America and a thematic interest in university governance, organizational change in higher education, and the development of the academic profession. Originally a lawyer, he also obtained a master's degree in public policy from Harvard University and a PhD in sociology of organizations from Boston University.

Jordan Brensinger served as a research intern for the Institute of International Education's Center for Academic Mobility Research. He is currently pursuing a master's in international affairs from at the School of International and Public Affairs, Columbia University. Brensinger has published and presented on themes of international higher education, and received the inaugural Comparative and International Education Society (CIES) Middle East Special Interest Group Student Paper Prize for his team's research on Egyptian higher education. Brensinger is also a member of the Comparative and International Education Society and the American Sociological Association. He obtained a BA in mathematics and Spanish from Messiah College and has traveled widely across Latin America.

Meghann Curtis serves as the Deputy Assistant Secretary for Academic Programs at the U.S. Department of State's Bureau of Educational and Cultural Affairs, where she oversees all academic programs sponsored by the Department, including the Fulbright Program, the Humphrey Program, the Gilman Program, Teacher Exchange Programs, and English Language Programs. She is also responsible for international student advising and marketing of American higher education resources through EducationUSA's network of 400 offices around the world. Curtis holds a master's degree in public affairs from Princeton University's Woodrow Wilson School of Public and International Affairs and a bachelor's degree from Vassar College.

Sylvie Didou Aupetit is a full-time researcher at the Center for Research and Advanced Studies, Mexico City, as well as head of a UNESCO Chair on Quality Assurance, Higher Education and New Providers of Educational Services in Latin America and Caribbean. She is also the general coordinator of the Observatory for Academic and Scientific Mobility (UNESCO). She has been a consultant for the Ford Foundation, UNESCO, the OECD, and the United Nations. She holds a PhD in linguistics and literature from Sorbonne University and another PhD in sociology from the School for Advanced Studies in the Social Sciences in Paris.

Oscar Espinoza is the director of the Center of Educational Research at the University of Informatics Sciences (UCINF) in Chile. He is also associate researcher at the Center of Comparative Educational Policies at University Diego Portales and in the Interdisciplinary Program of Educational Research. In addition, he works as a consultant for Chilean universities. In the past, he has worked in many research projects for international agencies (including USAID, UNESCO, the World Bank, UNDP, the Ford Foundation, and the Organization of Iberoamerican States) and national agencies (including the Ministry of Education of Chile and the National Commission for Scientific and Technological Research) in topics associated with access, equity, quality assurance, academic performance, accreditation, management, and higher education policies. He holds an EdD in policy, planning, and evaluation in education from the University of Pittsburgh.

Ana García de Fanelli is a senior researcher in higher education for the National Council of Research in Science and Technology (CONICET) and at the Center for the Study of State and Society (CEDES), Buenos Aires, Argentina. She is also a professor at the Universidad de Buenos Aires. She has published widely on comparative policies in higher education in Latin America, the management of public universities, and university financing. She holds a master's degree in the social sciences from the Latin American School of Social Sciences (FLACSO Buenos Aires) and a PhD in economics from the Universidad de Buenos Aires.

Neshani Jani is manager of communications and program development at the Institute of International Education, where she helps to develop proposals and assists with managing new communication and marketing initiatives. Previously, she worked as a research assistant at the Institute for Scientific Analysis and was a contributing writer at the Foreign Policy Association. Jani received an MA from New York University and a BA from the University of California, Davis.

Jonah Kokodyniak is deputy vice president of strategic development at the Institute of International Education, where he develops new programs and establishes partnerships with foundations, corporations, and government agencies. He also supervises IIE's fundraising initiatives. Previously, Kokodyniak was director of development for Global Kids, Inc., where he expanded the organization's reach, revenue, and activities. He has also worked on international education projects at The New School and Tufts University. Kokodyniak received an MA with Honors from the New School and a BA from the University of Vermont. He has also received training at the Columbia Business School and the MIT Sloan School of Management.

Lisa Kraus works as a special assistant for policy in the Office of Academic Programs in the Bureau of Educational and Cultural Affairs, U.S. Department of State. Kraus serves as a program officer and an adviser on policy matters related to academic programs, including bilateral strategic dialogues on higher education. Previously, she specialized in outreach to exchange program alumni for the Bureau. Kraus received her master's degree in international affairs from the Elliott School of International Affairs at The George Washington University and her bachelor's degree from Doane College in Crete, Nebraska. As a student, she studied abroad in Spain and Chile.

Jason E. Lane is director of policy research at the Nelson A. Rockefeller Institute of Government, the public policy think tank of the State University of New York (SUNY). He is also associate professor of educational policy, codirector of the Cross-Border Education Research Team, and senior researcher at the Institute for Global Education Policy Studies at the University at Albany, SUNY. His books include *Multinational Colleges and Universities* (with Kevin Kinser) and *Colleges and Universities as Economic Drivers* (with Bruce Johnstone). He serves on the boards of the Comparative and International Education Society, the Council for International Higher Education, and the Gulf Comparative Education Society.

Edward Monks is director, enrichment and professional development, at the Institute of International Education. He has overseen IIE's management of undergraduate programs, including the Brazil Scientific Mobility Program, the Study America Program, and placement for the LOTUS scholarship program. Monks oversees the management of IIE's visa sponsorship services for the Japanese Ministry of Education's Specialist Program, the College Board's Chinese Guest Teacher Program, and individual exchange programs for trainees, researchers, and short-term scholars. Prior to working at IIE, Monks taught English and writing in Argentina and for several years taught in the New York City region as an adjunct English as a second language (ESL) instructor. He is a graduate of Siena College in Albany in political science and international studies and also holds an MA in teaching ESL.

IIE Information and Resources

THE CENTER FOR INTERNATIONAL PARTNERSHIPS IN HIGHER EDUCATION

The IIE Center for International Partnerships in Higher Education draws on IIE's wide-ranging network of more than 1,100 colleges and universities and extensive expertise in international education to provide administrators, policymakers, and practitioners with the resources and connections to develop and sustain partnerships around the world. Major initiatives of the Center are the International Academic Partnerships Program and the IIE Global Partner Service. The Center also produces timely policy research and convenes international education leaders in conferences and workshops.

WEBSITE: www.iie.org/cip

THE CENTER FOR ACADEMIC MOBILITY RESEARCH

The IIE Center for Academic Mobility Research brings together the Institute's in-house research expertise with leading minds from around the world to conduct and disseminate timely and relevant research and policy analysis in the field of international student and faculty mobility. The Center provides applied research and program evaluation services to domestic and international governmental agencies, nongovernmental organizations, corporations, and foundations. The Center's in-depth books and reports, including the well-known *Open Doors Report on International Educational Exchange*, supported by the U.S. Department of State, are key reference resources. In addition, the Center's policy papers and snapshot surveys capture trends in the changing landscape of international education.

WEBSITE: www.iie.org/mobility

RECENT IIE WHITE AND BRIEFING PAPERS

IIE Papers address the changing landscape of international education, offering timely snapshots of critical issues in the field.

- Expanding U.S. Study Abroad to Brazil: A Guide for Institutions (2012)
- Models for U.S. Study Abroad to Indonesia (2012)
- U.S. and Australian International Student Data Collection: Key Differences and Practices (2012)
- Learn by Doing: Expanding International Internships/Work Abroad Opportunities for U.S. STEM Students (2012)
- English-Taught Master's Programs in Europe: New Findings on Supply and Demand (2012)
- U.S. Students in Overseas Degree Programs: Key Destinations and Fields of Study (2012)
- Joint and Double Degree Programs in a Global Context (September 2011)

- Expanding U.S. Study Abroad to India: A Guide for Institutions (July 2011)
- Evaluating and Measuring the Impact of Citizen Diplomacy: Current State and Future Directions (July 2011)
- Building Sustainable U.S.-Ethiopian University Partnerships: Findings from a Conference (July 2011)

WEBSITE: www.iie.org/publications

IIE/AIFS FOUNDATION GLOBAL EDUCATION RESEARCH REPORTS

This series of books explores the most pressing and underresearched issues affecting international education policy today.

- *Women in the Global Economy: Leading Social Change* (Forthcoming, March 2013)
- *Latin America's New Knowledge Economy: Higher Education, Government, and International Collaboration* (December 2011)
- *Developing Strategic International Partnerships: Models for Initiating and Sustaining Innovative Institutional Linkages* (October 2011)
- *Who Goes Where and Why? An Overview and Analysis of Global Educational Mobility* (April 2011)
- *Innovation through Education: Building the Knowledge Economy in the Middle East* (August 2010)
- *International India: A Turning Point in Educational Exchange with the U.S.* (January 2010)
- *Higher Education on the Move: New Developments in Global Mobility* (April 2009)
- *U.S.-China Educational Exchange: Perspectives on a Growing Partnership* (October 2008)

WEBSITE: www.iie.org/gerr

IIE Web Resources

IIEPASSPORT.ORG

This free online search engine lists nearly 10,000 study abroad programs worldwide and provides advisers with hands-on tools to counsel students and promote study abroad.

WEBSITE: www.iiepassport.org

STUDY ABROAD FUNDING

This valuable funding resource helps U.S. students find funding for study abroad programs.

WEBSITE: www.studyabroadfunding.org

FUNDING FOR UNITED STATES STUDY

This directory offers the most relevant data on hundreds of fellowships, grants, paid internships, and scholarships for study in the United States.

WEBSITE: www.fundingusstudy.org

INTENSIVE ENGLISH USA

Comprehensive reference with more than 500 accredited English language programs in the United States.

WEBSITE: www.intensiveenglishusa.org

FULBRIGHT PROGRAMS FOR U.S. STUDENTS

The Fulbright U.S. Student Program equips future American leaders with the skills they need to thrive in an increasingly global environment by providing funding for one academic year of study or research abroad, to be conducted after graduation from an accredited university.

SPONSOR: U.S. Department of State, Bureau of Educational and Cultural Affairs

WEBSITE: http://us.fulbrightonline.org

FULBRIGHT PROGRAMS FOR U.S. SCHOLARS

The traditional Fulbright Scholar Program sends hundreds of U.S. faculty and professionals abroad each year. Grantees lecture and conduct research in a wide variety of academic and professional fields.

SPONSOR: U.S. Department of State, Bureau of Educational and Cultural Affairs

WEBSITE: www.cies.org

Programs of the AIFS Foundation

The AIFS Foundation
The mission of the AIFS Foundation is to provide educational and cultural exchange opportunities to foster greater understanding among the people of the world. It seeks to fulfill this mission by organizing high-quality educational opportunities for students and providing grants to individuals and schools for participation in culturally enriching educational programs.

WEBSITE: www.aifsfoundation.org

ACADEMIC YEAR IN AMERICA (AYA)
Each year, AYA brings nearly 1,000 high school students from around the world to the United States. They come for the school year to live with American families and attend local high schools, learning about American culture and sharing their own languages and customs with their host families.

WEBSITE: www.academicyear.org

FUTURE LEADERS EXCHANGE PROGRAM (FLEX)
Established in 1992 under the FREEDOM Support Act and administered by the U.S. Department of State's Bureau of Educational and Cultural Affairs, FLEX encourages long-lasting peace and mutual understanding between the United States and the countries of Eurasia.

YOUTH EXCHANGE AND STUDY PROGRAM (YES)
Since 2002, this U.S. Department of State high school exchange program has enabled students from predominantly Muslim countries to learn about American society and values, acquire leadership skills, and help educate Americans about their countries and cultures.

Programs of the American Institute for Foreign Study

American Institute For Foreign Study
The AIFS mission is to enrich the lives of young people throughout the world by providing them with educational and cultural exchange programs of the highest possible quality.

WEBSITE: www.aifs.com

AIFS COLLEGE STUDY ABROAD
AIFS is a leading provider of study abroad programs for college students. Students can study abroad for a summer, semester, or academic year in 17 countries around the world. Faculty-led and customized programs are also offered.

WEBSITE: www.aifsabroad.com

AMERICAN COUNCIL FOR INTERNATIONAL STUDIES (ACIS)
For more than 30 years, ACIS has helped students and their teachers discover the world through premier travel and education. Teachers can choose destinations throughout Europe, the Americas, and Asia.

WEBSITE: www.acis.com

AU PAIR IN AMERICA
Au Pair in America makes it possible for nearly 4,000 eager and skilled young adults from around the world to join American families and help care for their children during a mutually rewarding, yearlong cultural exchange experience.

WEBSITE: www.aupairinamerica.com

CAMP AMERICA
Each summer, Camp America brings nearly 6,000 young people from around the world to the United States to work as camp counselors and camp staff.

WEBSITE: www.campamerica.aifs.com

CULTURAL INSURANCE SERVICES INTERNATIONAL (CISI)
CISI is the leading provider of study abroad and international student insurance coverage. Since 1992, CISI has insured more than 1 million international students and cultural exchange participants worldwide.

WEBSITE: www.culturalinsurance.com

SUMMER INSTITUTE FOR THE GIFTED (SIG)

SIG is a three-week academic, recreational, and social summer program for gifted and talented students. Students from around the world in grades 4 through 11 can participate in SIG Residential programs offered at university campuses across the country including Columbia University, Princeton University, Yale University, UC Berkeley, UCLA, Amherst College, Emory University, Bryn Mawr College, Vassar College, and University of Texas at Austin. Day, part-time and Saturday programs are also offered, as well as University Prep programs at selected institutions. SIG operates under the National Society for the Gifted and the Talented (NSGT), which is a nonprofit 501(c)3 organization.

WEBSITE: www.giftedstudy.org

AIFS Information and Resources

The following resources are available for download at www.aifsabroad.com/advisors/publications.asp

- Student Guide to Study Abroad and Career Development
- Diversity in International Education Summary Report
- The Gender Gap in Post-Secondary Study Abroad: Understanding and Marketing to Male Students
- Study Abroad: A 21st Century Perspective, Vol I
- Study Abroad: A 21st Century Perspective, Vol II: The Changing Landscape
- Innocents at Home Redux—The Continuing Challenge to America's Future
- Impact on Education Abroad on Career Development, Vol. I
- Impact on Education Abroad on Career Development: Four Community College Case Studies, Vol. II